The Complete
Handbook of
Science Fair
Projects

Related Titles of Interest from John Wiley & Sons

The Thomas Edison Book of Easy and Incredible Experiments, by The Thomas Alva Edison Foundation

Biology for Every Kid: 101 Easy Experiments that Really Work, by Janice Pratt VanCleave

Chemistry for Every Kid: 101 Easy Experiments that Really Work, by Janice Pratt VanCleave

Earth Science for Every Kid: 101 Experiments that Really Work, by Janice Pratt VanCleave

Clouds in a Glass of Beer: Simple Experiments in Atmospheric Physics, by Craig F. Bohren

What Light Through Yonder Window Breaks? More Experiments in Atmospheric Physics, by Craig F. Bohren

Seeing the Sky: 100 Projects, Activities and Explorations in Astronomy, by Fred Schaaf

Touring the Universe through Binoculars: A Complete Astronomer's Guidebook, by Philip S. Harrington

Nature for the Very Young: A Handbook of Indoor and Outdoor Activities, by Marcia Bowden

The Naturalist's Year: 24 Outdoor Explorations, by Scott Camazine

The Complete Handbook of Science Fair Projects

JULIANNE BLAIR BOCHINSKI

Wiley Science Editions

John Wiley & Sons, Inc.

NEW YORK • CHICHESTER • BRISBANE • TORONTO • SINGAPORE

Library of Congress Cataloging-in-Publication Data
Bochinski, Julianne Blair, 1966–
    The complete handbook of science fair projects / Julianne Blair Bochinski.
        p. cm. — (Wiley science editions)
    Includes index.
    Summary: Discusses various aspects of science fairs and science fair projects including advice on choosing a topic, doing research, developing experiments, organizing data results, and presenting a project to the judges.
    ISBN 0–471–52729–7 (c). — ISBN 0–471–52728–9 (p)
    1. Science projects—Handbooks, manuals, etc.—Juvenile literature. [1. Science projects—Handbooks, manuals, etc. 2. Handbooks, manuals, etc.] I. Title. II. Series.
Q182.3.B63   1991
507.9—dc20   90–42621

Printed in the United States of America

91 92 10 9 8 7 6 5 4

To my father—Edmund J. Bochinski

With gratitude and respect
for his counseling, care, and
inimitable sense of humor and wit.

"vir et consili magni et benefici"
—Ego te saluto!

Love, Jules

Acknowledgments

This book, the product of four years of writing, consulting, editing, collecting dust, and writing again would not exist if it were not for the interest of some very honorable people from the scientific community. I am privileged to have received the support and invaluable suggestions of the directors, committee members and judges of the Connecticut Science Fair Association, Inc., and I am indebted to two of these individuals in particular.

Many thanks are due Mr. George Robert Wisner, for his advice and tireless dedication in editing the early stages of this book and for making me a part of one of the most respected science fairs in the country. Mr. Wisner is the Chairman of the Board of Directors at the Connecticut Science Fair Association, Inc., and has devoted much of his time and talent over the last 15 years to organizing this successful annual event. He has coordinated science fair workshops statewide and has provided many educational opportunities for the youth of Connecticut.

Acknowledgment is also due to Sister Mary Christine, for her recognition of the need for the material I had written, and for her tremendous assistance and advice in the sample science fair projects section. Sister Christine holds the position of Secretary of the Connecticut Science Fair Board of Directors and also directs one of the Fair's committees. As chairperson of the mathematics department at Mary Immaculate Academy in New Britain, Connecticut, Sister Christine is also respected throughout the Greater New Britain area as a devoted mentor to children pursuing science fair projects.

I would also like to express my gratitude to Science Service in Washington, D.C., for their advice and providing me with the listings of the state, regional, and foreign science fairs. As a nonprofit institution, Science Service is dedicated to providing educational programs in science for students around the world. They also administer the International Science and Engineering Fair.

In addition, a special thank you goes out to my sister, Judith J. Bochinski-DiBiase, a professional designer, for executing the book illustrations in the crazy and hilarious late-night hours of May and June.

Finally, I am grateful to my godfather William J. Lyons for his continued support in this and many other endeavors in my education.

Student Consultants

A very talented group of young scientists deserves an extra special acknowledgment for their ideas and input for some of the science fair projects that appear in the sample science fair projects section. These students are:

- Eduardo Federico Canedo, "Does the Period of Motion of a Pendulum Depend on Its Weight, Amplitude, or Length?"
- Hillary Charnas, "The Effects of Gender Identity on Short-Term Memory"
- Natalie Ciesielski, "Can Ocean Waves Be Used to Generate Electricity?"
- George F. Claffey, "What Section of a Town Has the Most Pollution in the Form of Airborne Particles?"
- Amy Concilio, "What Colored Dyes Are Found in Powdered Drink Mix and Colored Markers?"
- Brian J. Curtin, "Are Your Clams Safe to Eat?"
- Henry Fiedorczyk, "The Robotic-Assisted Plotter"
- Kyle Fischer, "The Effects of Industrial Pollutants on the Environment of the Convict Cichlid Fish"
- Kirsten B. Glass, "How Effective Is Lobster Shell Chitin in Filtering Wastewater Metallic Ions?"
- Michelle Harris, "Polarization and Stress Analysis of Airplane Windows"
- Kristin Hertzig, "Are Dogs Colorblind?"
- Adam K. Horelik, "Do All Plants Transpire at the Same Rate Under Different Sources of Light?"
- Sara Horesco, "What Colored Dyes Are Found in Powdered Drink Mix and Colored Markers?"
- David A. Karanian, "The Relationship Between Alcohol Dosage and Dependency in a Rat"
- Albert Kim, "Which Angle of Attack Generates the Most Lift?"

- Theresa Konicki, "How Can the Amount of Bacteria Found on Kitchen Sponges and Dishrags Be Reduced?"
- Cathy Magliocco, "Can Limestone Be Used to Protect Pine Trees from Acid Rain?"
- Jodi Marak, "How Does Acid Rain Affect the Cell Structure of *Spirogyra*?"
- Kathy Mikk, "How Does Saltwater Mix in an Estuary?"
- Meredith Miller, "The Effects of Gender Identity on Short-Term Memory"
- Christina L. Olson, "Environmental Effects on the Biodegradability of Plastic Bags, Paper Bags, and Newspaper"
- Celeste N. Peterson, "Can the Heartbeat of a Chicken Embryo Be Detected Without Breaking Its Eggshell?"
- Mira Rho, "How Effective Are Various Items in Protecting Against Ultraviolet Radiation?"
- Jason Riha, "Are Composites of Wood Stronger than Solid Wood?"
- Cathy Rion, "How Do Different Surfaces Affect the Distance Mealworms Travel in 2 Minutes?"
- Laura Sharpe, "What Is the Effect of #6 Heating Oil on *Elodea densa* in an Aquatic Environment?"
- Stanley W. Shostak, "Can CMOS Logic, Rather than a Potentiometer, Regulate Voltage?"
- Christina Smilnak, "Can Plant Cloning Be Used Effectively by Produce Growers?"
- Robert Smith, "An Analysis of the Bacteria and Heavy Metal Content in Sewage Before and After Treatment at a Sewage Plant"
- Margaret Stanek, "How Effective Is Beta Carotene in Fighting Cancer in Plants?"
- Susan Thibeault, "The Effects of Hard and Soft Water Respiration from an Ultrasonic Humidifier on Mealworms"
- Karen Thickman, "The Effect of Electromagnetic Fields on *Eremosphaera* Algae Cells"
- Connie W. Tsao, "Shape and Viscous Effect"
- Betsy Ruth Velasco, "What Substance Is Most Effective in Preventing the Breeding of Bacteria in Water Beds?"
- Christopher Waluk, "Footwear versus Bacteria"
- John Wasielewski, "What Would Happen to Climate, Weather Patterns, and Life Forms if the Earth Were Cubical?"
- Joseph Wasielewski, "Can the Life Span of a Soap Bubble Be Extended in Different Temperatures and Atmospheric Conditions?"
- Thaddeus A. Wojtusik, "Common Cold Remedies: Are They Helpful?"

International Science and Engineering Fair Alumni

♦ Katherine Frances Orzel, "The P-Trap: A Bacteria Cauldron" and "The P-Trap: A Continuing Dilemma"

♦ Matthew Green, "The Wave, the Golden Mean,
and $r = \left[\dfrac{2}{(-1 + \sqrt{5})} \right]^{\wedge} \theta$"

♦ Damon O. Kheir-Eldin, "Improving the Antibacterial Effects of Garlic"

Preface

Science is a means for improving the quality of human life and technology. Almost everything you use to make your life easier can be credited to science: a need had developed, a mind was alerted, and through a process of experimentation, a solution was discovered that made its scientific mark on the world.

It is through scientific effort that many talented people have and will continue to discover important facts, including someone such as yourself. Your knowledge and curiosity in the many fields of science is greatly needed in our rapidly changing world. Because of this need, many science-related opportunities will await you by the time you graduate from college. Careers in research, engineering, and teaching will be available if you start preparing now.

From the local to the international level, science fairs are a fun way to gather science experience while you pursue an independent project. They are in many ways the roads to opportunity and success. In fact, many of today's most respected doctors and engineers completed science fair projects when they were your age.

Whether you are a first-timer or a somewhat experienced science student, this book will introduce you to every aspect of science fairs and science fair projects. This book will show you the shortcuts to finding a suitable topic and learning how to research it properly; how to develop a meaningful experiment; and how to organize your data results easily. This book will also give you guidelines and suggestions for an attractive display, together with tips for presenting your project to a panel of judges, and a look at what goes on behind the scenes.

The appendices contain a wealth of practical information, with over 400 suggested science project topics; the names and locations of many state and regional science fairs in and out of the United States; the names, addresses, and phone numbers of 40 scientific supply companies across the country; and—perhaps of most importance to any student, the titles and outlines of 50 recent, award-winning state science fair projects that will serve as models for successful science fair projects on different grade levels.

By using this book, you should find your science fair project easier to organize and present, and your contribution to the field of science more meaningful. Remember, in order for society to continue to grow and understand the world around it, it will need a new generation of scientific know-how and talent. So, hats off to you! May the following pages help you reach your ultimate goal—that someday you, too, will make your own scientific mark on the world.

SI (Metric) Conversion Table

Both the English and the SI (Metric) systems of measurement have been used in this book to simplify the student's understanding of specialized experimental procedures and the measurement-specific scientific instruments discussed.

	English	Symbol	= (SI) Metric	Symbol
Length				
	1 inch	in	2.54 centimeters	cm
	1 foot	ft	30.00 centimeters	cm
	1 yard	yd	0.90 meters	m
	1 mile	mi	1.60 kilometers	km
Mass				
	1 ounce	oz	28.00 grams	g
	1 pound	lb	0.45 kilograms	kg
Volume				
	1 teaspoon	tsp	5.00 milliliters	ml
	1 tablespoon	tbsp	15.00 milliliters	ml
	1 fluid ounce	fl oz	30.00 milliliters	ml
	1 cup	c	0.24 liters	l
	1 pint	pt	0.47 liters	l
	1 quart	qt	0.95 liters	l
	1 gallon	gal	3.80 liters	l

Temperature

Water freezes at:
    32 degrees Fahrenheit   °F   0 degrees Celsius   °C

Water boils at:
    212 degrees Fahrenheit   100 degrees Celsius

Normal human body temperature:
    98.6 degrees Fahrenheit   37 degrees Celsius

To convert Fahrenheit to Celsius:

$$(°F - 32) \times \tfrac{5}{9}$$

To convert Celsius to Fahrenheit:

$$\frac{°C + 32}{\tfrac{5}{9}}$$

Contents

xvi

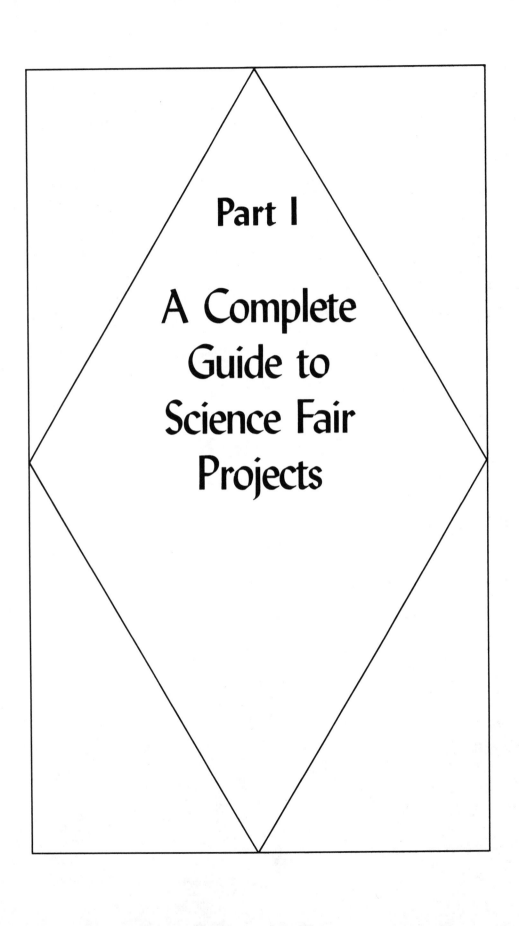

Part I

A Complete Guide to Science Fair Projects

Chapter 1 ——————————

Introduction:
From Popcorn to
Moonshine—My Early
Science Fair Experiences

I will never forget my first science fair project experience. I was in the sixth grade at the time and the project I had presented made me feel more like an amateur cook than an aspiring young scientist. "What Makes Popcorn Pop?" was the title of my project and looking back on it, I can now say that it would have been more appropriate at a cooking exhibition than at a science fair.

The science fair project was a required assignment for all students at St. Francis Middle School, and it seemed to create a lot of uncertainty, especially to first-timers. Like my fellow classmates, I did not have any idea of what a science project was supposed to do or even look like. In fact, the closest I had ever come to seeing one was a homemade volcano that Peter Brady had constructed in a "Brady Bunch" episode. So, reduced to a state of utter confusion, I tried to scrape up anything that could get me through the crisis.

What is a backboard? How do I go about researching my project? How do I develop my topic through experimentation? These were just a few of my many questions. I wished there had been a guide to science fair projects available at that time to explain the golden rules of what needed to be done.

But as it turned out, I made it through the crisis, and my popcorn presentation was a hit! . . . that is, a hit as a concession stand for hungry viewers. The crowd seemed to follow their noses through the door to my Sears Roebuck deluxe hot air popcorn popper, which was making popcorn for every demonstration. I stood beside my backboard, explaining that when a kernel is heated to a certain temperature, the expansion of the moisture inside will cause it to explode. I sounded like a broken record. My observers simply kept on crunching mouthful after mouthful of popped corn. I knew that I had chosen the wrong topic when someone asked if I had any hot melted butter.

Actually, there was nothing wrong with my topic. I had presented a question that could be answered in a scientific way. But what was inappropriate was the lack of scientific thought and creativity in the project. With a little guidance, I could have made further investigations into the nature of popping corn and its characteristics. For example, I could have collected several specimens of corn for study and shown the variation that exists among them. I could also have proven why popcorn was different from other types of corn and how temperature and humidity levels in the environment affect its performance. Perhaps I could have called it "An Examination of Environmental Conditions Influencing Moisture Potentials of Various Grades of Popcorn." To make a long story short, this elementary idea could have been turned into a genuine scientific investigation rather than a summary of facts and a make-shift demonstration.

The following year I was determined to find the makings of an ideal science project. One day at the beginning of the school year I decided to begin my search. The fair was four months away, and I had plenty of time to do a thorough job. I went to my local library and started to look through engineering textbooks and technical encyclopedias for the ideal project. Every day for nearly a week I spent hours searching for the most impressive scientific topic I could, in books that were far beyond my seventh grade science level. Not only was I aiming for first place this time, but also for the best science fair project in my school's history! Despite my ambition, however, I never found a topic. All the books seemed mean and intimidating and they were all written in the same language: "The woosawig is technically the engineered erfnogin of the state-of-the-art schmooziloogel." At some point I think one of the books bit me, and from then on I realized the contenders in the fight for science project supremacy would be me versus the public library.

After my fruitless search at the library, my dreams of a successful project vanished. I sulked for weeks until the day when I noticed that only a month was left before the school science fair. I broke into a cold sweat, realizing that I had nothing to show for my long quest for truth and answers. So I did what any self-respecting seventh-grader would do in a "scholastic 911"—I consulted the wisdom of the old, great, omniscient one—Dad.

My Dad told me to relax and assured me that I would eventually come up with something. "Just give it a little more time" he said, "there is a topic out there, and the two of you just have to get together." My father then gave me a news article that he thought I might like to read. Feeling as though I were getting nowhere, I took the article to my room and began to read it. The title of the article was, "Fluoride—Panacea or Poison?," and it looked interesting, for a change. As I continued to read it I found myself unusually involved in its argument. It made me wonder whether the chemical that was in my local drinking water and my toothpaste was indeed a "tooth-decay preventer" as some people claimed. I

4

began to think about whether the fluoride that was supposedly protecting my teeth was at the same time doing other things to the rest of my bodily tissues, since the fluoridated water that I drank did not only stay in my mouth, but also traveled through the rest of me. Nevertheless, while I found this interesting, I feared that it was really wasting time. Or was it? I later realized that this article would be the basis for a great topic, and thus the fluoridation project emerged. (Do you think my dad knew something?)

I submitted the fluoride project to the school fair on time and ended up with an honorable mention and recognition from a local health group. But most importantly, I acquired a great deal of knowledge that I would not have obtained otherwise. Maybe this was not my "science project extraordinaire," but at least it gave me the determination to do an even better job the following year.

In my final year of junior high school, I came across a topic while watching an old black and white movie about the ancient Egyptian pyramids. I was so stunned by the size and perfection of the pyramids that I soon began researching them as a topic. I learned that when pyramids are built to precise measurements, they may actually give off a magnetic effect. I also read that some people claim that pyramids are capable of sharpening a razor blade, preserving a flower, and energizing water, provided these items are placed correctly inside the pyramids. These statements seemed so incredible to me that I decided to construct my own pyramid to see what it could do.

My pyramid was made of plexi-glass, and was about the size of a hat box. I had carefully cut the glass to form a 53 degree slope (the measurement required for magnetic power to be present) and glued the pieces together. Finally the pyramid was complete and I was ready to become a firm believer in its mysterious powers and amaze my friends and family.

However, after several days of uneventful experimentation, I was crushed. My magnetically mysterious pyramid turned out to be a big flop! None of the experiments worked like the authors of the textbooks had promised. I was stuck three weeks prior to the school fair with no project, a plexi-glass conversation piece, and a dead flower. It was much too late to look for a new topic, so I had to make do with what I had. I wrote a report and constructed a backboard based on information I copied from the pyramid books. I listed the experiments the author gave and fudged my experimental results so that the pyramid would look legitimate. Actually, despite its less than honest results, the pyramid project did not look so bad after all. Besides, how would anyone know that it was a sham? Believe it or not, I fooled everyone and captured the first place in my grade level. I was also on my way to the state science fair competition.

The state science fair was more exciting than I had expected. Most of the exhibits there demonstrated to me what a well-researched project was, how a topic could be developed through experimentation, and what a backboard was supposed to look like. I spent the whole week at the fair (even though I was not a finalist), studying and photographing every aspect of the winning projects. I walked away from the 1981 Connecticut Science Fair with a brand new concept of what a science project was supposed to be. This was the information that I had been looking for since my "popcorn project." Also, the notions of scientific thought and creativity acquired new meanings for me, as I pondered the fact that one cannot con a science fair judge into believing made-up results from experiments with a stubborn pyramid. But most importantly, I learned that I did not have to fudge my data in order to salvage my flopped experiment. My project would have probably earned more points if I had noted its true results and made an attempt to identify and remove those variables that interfered with the pyramid's operation.

After three years of experience, I felt that I had built up a solid background for science fair projects. I was sure that my first year in Mary Immaculate Academy High School was going to be my year to shine. I was excited when I found out that my science instructor and mentor, Sister Mary Christine, was affiliated with the Connecticut Science Fair as a chairperson. At the time, my teacher had placed an average of three finalists every year at the state science fair in both the senior physical and biological divisions. Rumor had it that she expected nothing but the best from her freshman class.

Before the school year began, I found a topic that really interested me. The United States was in the midst of an energy crisis, and I selected a relevant topic: "Alcohol as a Fuel . . . Recycling Wastes into Energy." This was my best science project so far, and I could fill an entire book describing what I accomplished and learned with this topic. This project was different from the others because I applied scientific thought and creativity to a novel approach and had the experience of past competitions. I was now aware of what the judges were looking for, and I had every intention of fulfilling their expectations.

This time there were no unsuccessful searches in the public library or fake experiments. After I obtained a permit from the Bureau of Alcohol Tobacco and Firearms to produce homemade ethanol, I knew where to acquire the information I would need for my research. I also had the supervision of an engineer as I was constructing the still in which to manufacture alcohol. It was my objective to prove that alcohol was a more effective fuel than either oil or gasoline. My teachers and classmates, however, felt that they knew a better use for the alcohol, as they repeatedly asked me for a bottle of moonshine!

To make the alcohol, I first had to make a mash. This mixture consisted of apple peelings, water and yeast. I allowed the mash to ferment for a week in a dark furnace room and turn into beer. After this was done, I transferred the beer into my homemade still and distilled it into alcohol. The distillation process went rather well, except for the fact that my family became a little lightheaded from the fumes. After I had achieved the highest concentration of alcohol possible from my still, I set up several

The author's project as it appeared in 1982 at the
Connecticut Science Fair.

controls and found that the alcohol I had produced was a remarkably
efficient fuel compared with oil, kerosene, and gasoline. In fact, the alcohol proved to be such a good fuel that I was able, with the help of my
father, to adjust the carburetor on my family's lawn mower to burn alcohol instead of gasoline. My project placed first in my school, and once
again I found myself headed for the Connecticut Science Fair.

That year was very successful for myself and for other students at
my school, which had a total of five finalists. In addition to being a finalist in the regular awards portion of the fair, I also received awards from
the SEER (Student Exposition on Energy Resources) group, the Society of
Women Engineers, and the Junior Engineering Technical Society. While
I did not make first place in my division, I came close. It was certainly a
better experience than the science fairs of preceding years.

However, my science fair days were not over yet. Instead of competing, I volunteered at the Connecticut Science Fair as an assistant to my

science instructor. Today, I judge as well as manage the awards portion of the state fair. Although my days of competing are now over, I still enjoy participating in the state fair and advising the excited contestants. I know it is a great feeling to have those months of your dedicated work rewarded by being selected as a finalist. It is an even greater feeling to know that you have acquired useful experience in a particular scientific field and to have contributed by means of that experience to the scientific community.

So, if you think that a "popcorn-type project" is just about what you're capable of doing right now, don't worry! The important thing to remember is that you are not alone, because this handbook will be your coach and personal advisor as you make your way through the process of completing and submitting a science fair project. While you may have laughed at my adventure in quest of the ideal science project, I hope that you have already learned from this account of some of the mistakes I made. Success will not happen overnight, but eventually you too will find the ideal science fair project.

Chapter 2———————————————

Science Fairs and Science Fair Projects

WHAT IS A SCIENCE FAIR?

Many schools present science fairs after their students have completed a group of science projects. These fairs are public exhibitions of the students' projects to provide recognition for their work and to stimulate interest in science. Professionals from the scientific community often judge the science projects according to commonly accepted scientific standards.

If you participate in a science fair you may compete for prizes and for the chance to move on to a higher competition in a state or regional fair, or to the highest level in the International Science and Engineering Fair. One of the most important aspects of science fairs is that they give you educational opportunities for exchanging and learning new scientific methods and concepts with professionals and other contestants. (See Appendix C for a complete listing of all state, regional, and foreign fairs affiliated with the International Science and Engineering Fair.)

WHAT IS A SCIENCE FAIR PROJECT?

A science project gives you the opportunity to gain hands-on experience and knowledge in an independent field of study. It is a challenging, extracurricular assignment that allows you to use your own ideas or a topic provided by your instructor to investigate scientific problems that interest you.

Each year, hundreds of students enter state, regional, or foreign affiliates of the International Science and Engineering Fair.

The Scientific Method

It seems only fair to set forth the component parts of a science fair project by giving you a few definitions before you plan your first project.

A science project is your attempt to study a scientific problem in order to answer a proposed question or develop a better technique or final product. Science projects primarily involve research and tests to arrive at a specific conclusion. The basic procedure involved in science projects is modeled on a process called **the scientific method.** This method consists of the following elements: purpose, hypothesis, research, experiment, and conclusion. Each element may be defined as follows:

> *Purpose.* The problem or question for which you are seeking a solution. (*Example: Does an interrupted sleeping pattern affect alertness?*)

> *Hypothesis.* Your educated guess about the solution to the question. (*Example: I believe that sleep influences one's alertness.*)

Research. The process by which you gather information by consulting libraries, instructors, professionals, or scientific organizations. Also, the period for planning and organizing your experiment.

Experiment. The process by which you develop your subject knowledge and research findings into tests. (*Example: Two groups of people will be studied. Group I will be allowed to sleep 9 hours without interruption. Group II will be allowed to sleep 10 hours and will be awakened every 2 hours for 15 minutes to give group members a total of 9 hours sleep. Following the periods of sleep, both groups will be tested for alertness to determine whether their performance is influenced by the conditions they were subjected to prior to the test.*)

Conclusion. The solution to your proposed question and proof or disproof of your hypothesis. (*Example: Based on the data from this test, interrupted sleepers perform less efficiently than noninterrupted ones on a standard alertness test.*)

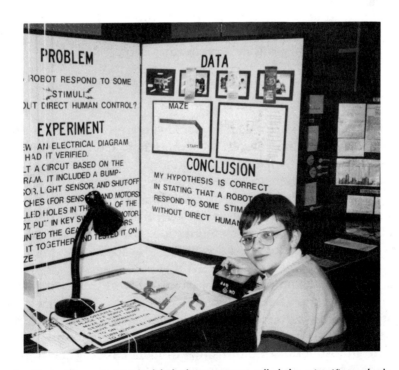

A science fair project is modeled after a system called the scientific method.

Chapter 3

Getting Started

SELECT A TOPIC

Believe it or not, selecting a topic for a science project is the toughest part of the process for some students. Every year many students who plan to do a science fair project begin the usual library search through volumes and volumes of scientific literature without knowing what they are looking for. After several useless attempts at finding information, most students end up by quitting in frustration. The fact is not that the library is not a good place to find a topic, but that most students are not organized when they begin their search for a topic.

Think About Your Interests

The first step in getting organized is picking an area of science in which you have some particular interest or experience. One suggestion is to make a list of general science categories that you like. Then, go through your list and classify each category into subcategories of interest. For example, if one of the categories you listed was *health,* some subcategories might include *nutrition, diet,* and *vitamins.* Chances are good that you will find yourself more interested in one area than in another. Such preferences usually indicate good possibilities for topics. If, for example, you chose *vitamins* as your subject, you should then try to identify a particular aspect of vitamins that you want to investigate. Do you want to study the effects a particular vitamin has in alleviating arthritis, or do you want to see how it functions as a supplement with certain foods? If you chose *birds* as your subject, you should determine whether you want to study the atmospheric conditions that influence their migration, or to see how atmospheric conditions affect their life span. These are just a few examples of how you would develop a topic from your selected subject area (see Appendix A).

Remember that your best choice for a topic is a subject in which you have a particular interest. While it is helpful to have some knowledge of the topic before you choose it, this is not essential. If you are interested and resourceful, you will learn what you need to know. Remember, there is nothing worse than to be unhappy with your topic. Do not be afraid to get out of it and find another topic if you do happen to become bored or disinterested with your original choice.

Think About Your Experiences

Another means of selecting a topic is by examining your past experiences. Ask yourself whether you remember any unusual experiences in your life. For example, perhaps you once felt that your eyesight would improve whenever you ate a certain vegetable, or perhaps you discovered a rare type of moss growing on a tree stump in your backyard. You also may have wondered whether the material that enabled your watch dial to glow in the dark also emitted radiation that was affecting your environment. Personal experiences such as these are excellent sources for you to get project ideas.

Research Science Abstracts

Another possible source for a good topic is scientific abstracts. Abstracts can be located in bound scientific journals that are usually available at your local college or university libraries. These specialized journals are used primarily by science professionals. Articles are generally grouped into two classes: research experimental reports and reviews of scientific literature. Monthly issues are published in accordance with a cumulative subject and author index that is published annually.

Research Periodicals

Another area to investigate if you have not already thought of a topic are the periodicals in your field of interest. Go to your local library and look through the most recent magazines and newsletters in the field you have chosen. These are effective aids in finding and researching a topic because they are concise and up-to-date. Magazines such as *National Geographic, Discover, Popular Science, Popular Mechanics, Mother Earth News, Scientific American, High Technology* and *Prevention Health Magazine* are some of the best journals to consult while searching for an original topic.

Research Current Topics

Keep in mind, too, that a successful project tends to be one that employs a new technology, current issue, or novel approach. For example, in the late 1970s and early 1980s, the main public concern of many Americans was the energy issue, so projects that involved energy themes fared well. You can often find topics on the latest issues by reading periodical journals and scientific abstracts.

Read This Book

Another way to get ideas for a topic and to see how a topic is developed is by scanning the top projects at the next local or state science fair. For your convenience, this handbook contains the outlines of 50 award-winning projects, including several projects that were candidates in the International Science and Engineering Fair (ISEF). The outlines will describe the materials these finalists used, their objectives, and the experimental procedures they followed. The actual findings were left out and questions were added in their place, so that you may use these projects as models and draw your own conclusions. The projects were not intended to do the work for you, but rather to give you an idea of how topics can be developed.

ORGANIZE YOUR INVESTIGATION

Once you have found a topic that satisfies you, you are ready to get started. At this time, it is necessary to reorganize yourself and take inventory. You can begin by getting a notebook to create a journal of everything that you will be learning and doing on your project. A journal often proves to be the most efficient way of organizing your research and what's more is that it will serve as an excellent outline for your report. Describe in your journal articles you have read, places you have visited, data results, and other points you think are worth noting. Write down important information so that you will not have to search through past references again.

As a researcher, you are investigating a particular problem or question. It would be helpful to know exactly what you are aiming for and how far you are willing to go to pursue your immediate objective. Before you get started, take into consideration the amount of time you have to complete the project, plan it accordingly, and—most importantly—find out if certain conditions limit you or your topic.

Project Limitation Guidelines

Guidelines established by the International Science and Engineering Fair will govern your research and experimentation. This means that you may have to work with a qualified professional or obtain a permit from a particular agency. Some of the areas in which strict rules apply involve vertebrate animals, human subjects, recombinant DNA, and human and animal tissues. All uses of animals in research and experimentation must be performed humanely and with respect to the animal's well-being. This restriction even applies to observations of animals in their natural habitat. The ISEF encourages the use of **protista** and other invertebrates for animal research because of their wide availability. However, if your topic involves higher forms of animals, you must be extremely careful and conscientious in all experiments. You will need a qualified and knowledgeable scientist to advise you on caring for and using the animal in compliance with local, state, and federal laws. The same rules apply to human subjects. (When working with DNA and body tissues, only research that is normally conducted in a microbiological laboratory is acceptable. Specimens must be obtained from a qualified scientist whom your teacher can recommend. The ISEF defines a qualified scientist as "an individual who possesses an earned doctoral degree in science or medicine, and who has a working knowledge of the techniques to be used by a student in his or her research plan.")

Controlled substances such as drugs, chemicals, and alcohol have certain restrictions and requirements that must be met before experimentation. Other questionable areas include the use of lasers, radioactive material, and high voltage equipment. As always, check with your advisor or the official rule book of the ISEF before beginning your experiment to find out if you need assistance or certification to work on the topic you have chosen.

BEGIN YOUR RESEARCH

A good way to begin work on your topic is by checking all relevent periodicals and scientific abstracts at your library. Most current scientific articles list additional sources of cross-references at the end of their reports. Some give the names and addresses of organizations and people who can supply more information, such as area groups, universities, or technicians. Take advantage of these helpful references because they are your best source for up-to-date facts.

As soon as you think you have located some useful addresses, write a letter to the organization or person mentioned in your article or cross-reference. State that you are a student working under a deadline, and discuss the plans you have in mind for your project and the information you will need to gather. Ask for all available literature and any suggestions for experimentation. Also, ask for additional references of persons in your area who are working in this field.

Make several copies of this letter and send them to the people and organizations who may be able to help you. Most people will be glad to help, especially if it relates to their own ideas or products. Sending out such letters enables you to save time by eliminating useless searches and limiting your information to the details that you need. Remember, you can always refer to textbooks, periodicals, and scientific abstracts when you need additional information.

Printed below is the letter I sent to a few energy groups requesting information on alcohol as an alternative energy resource. This letter resulted in my receiving four informational guides that helped me through my entire project. Along with the guides, I received lists containing the titles of exclusive literature on my subject and the address of an alcohol fuel producer who lived in my county.

Julianne Bochinski
Mary Immaculate Academy
New Britain, CT 06053

September 1, 1981

Renewable Energy Information
P.O. Box 8900
Silver Spring, MD 20907

Dear Director:

I am a high school student currently working on a science project for the Connecticut Science Fair. My project concerns the recycling of fermented organic garbage into ethyl alcohol. My objective is to see if it is possible for a household to construct a simple and inexpensive still capable of producing enough alcohol fuel to meet the household's energy needs. I also plan to compare ethyl alcohol with other natural fuel sources to determine its efficiency.

Recently, I found your address in an alcohol fuel directory. This guide mentioned that your organization would be able to assist ethyl alcohol fuel producers by providing them with suggestions and further information.

At this time, I would be grateful for any current information on alcohol production, still designs, and alcohol producers in my area. If possible, please send this information to me soon since I am working toward a February deadline.

If all goes well, this will be both an informative and stimulating project for me and my community.

Sincerely,

Julianne Bochinski

SUMMARY

1. Select a topic by focusing on an area that interests you and by identifying a specific category for a project.

2. Identify what you are looking for and how far you are willing to go to pursue your immediate objective. (This includes checking with your advisor and the guidelines established by the ISEF for specific rules and regulations.)

3. Create a journal of important points in your research.

4. Research periodicals and scientific abstracts for cross-references and addresses to contact organizations or persons in your subject area.

5. Write a letter and send copies of it to each of the groups you have selected.

Chapter 4

Conducting an Experiment

The experiment can either make or break your science project. This is the backbone of the project, and it is essential that you put sufficient thought and preparation into it. Thus, you should plan to spend most of your time on a feasible experiment after researching. After all, this is where you contribute your own ideas and creative ability.

Your experiment should encompass everything that you have learned about your topic. Your research should be applied to a practical application that involves measurements, analyses, or tests to answer a

The experiment is perhaps the most important part of a science fair project.

specific question. Judges look for these individual qualities and will be distracted if your project contains irrelevant facts and data.

Make sure that the work you do is an experiment. Judges all too often see projects that are researched thoroughly and presented in a neat, attractive manner, only to find that their experiments merely involve a presentation of a well-known idea, or a display that the public has seen too many times. Such exhibits are not experiments, but mere demonstrations. While preparing your project, try to present a question and then prepare a series of tests to solve the problem or support a proposed hypothesis. If you follow the scientific method (see Chapter 2), your project should be easier to complete and will provide more meaningful results than if you do not use this method.

Because you will want your results to be absolutely accurate, you should record all your data, regardless of whether or not they support your hypothesis. Your project will not be scored low or disqualified simply because your results did not support your hypothesis. You may develop your project by interpreting your end results and explaining why they were different than what you had expected.

Keep in mind that judges do not expect you to come up with a revolutionary idea. They are more interested in seeing how much scientific skill and thought you applied to your project. Most projects have been done before in one form or another. They usually differ according to the extent that they are applied techniques of an original idea, or a confirmation of a conclusion under varying circumstances. Some contestants even submit the same project in a following science fair because they have made significant progress in their topics since their first entry.

DEFINE YOUR OBJECTIVE

Before you begin, it is essential that you streamline your proposed question. Decide what it is that you want to prove and try to attack the most important aspect of your topic. For example, if you choose toxic waste as your topic, you would probably research its hazardous byproducts, clean-up solutions, and future outlook. Such a broad topic would yield a variety of details without a specific focus or purpose. It should be clear that you must confine your topic to a single purpose or question. This can be done by listing all the different approaches that may be taken in your project through experimentation. Some of these might include:

1. Determining the effects that industrially contaminated waste has on the growth of organisms.
2. Comparing health and disease statistics between different toxic waste sites.
3. Determining the efficiency of a proposed solution to neutralize toxic waste.

After you have listed various approaches to your project, choose one that you think will produce a reasonable and practical experiment.

Given these choices, the second alternative would probably be too broad to work with. Such an experiment would require several years in order for you to compare the health and disease characteristics of several sites. The work would involve periodic studies of people, animals, and plants, in order to measure their endurance, immunity, and quality of vital functions. Although this is a very challenging idea, it would be too general to satisfy your immediate objective. The third alternative would be a great experiment if you had access to a new toxic waste solution, such as a chemical that would act as a stabilizer in eliminating byproducts. You could measure the efficiency of this chemical in order to find out which by-products it could break down. However, this project would be too diverse to satisfy your immediate objective, and would pose a problem if you did not already have a solution in mind.

In general, the second and third alternatives seem to be too broad for your purposes. The first topic probably would be the best choice, because it focuses on one central idea—the effects of toxic waste on growth. A procedural plan could easily be developed to parallel your purpose.

ORGANIZE YOUR EXPERIMENT

Once you have decided on an experimental approach, you must organize an experiment. In the example regarding toxic waste, you must organize an experiment that will allow you to measure growth in the presence of industrially contaminated waste. It would be difficult to measure human or animal growth in a short time period, so a more practical subject would be a plant. Since you may not detect any noticeable difference in growth by merely placing the plant in the presence of toxic waste, you may decide instead to place the plant (*Coleus,* for example) in various samples of contaminated soil from different manufacturing and dumping sites. Your objective would then be to study the effects of toxic soil on the growth of a *Coleus* plant. After you have organized your experiment, a procedural plan must be developed.

CREATE A PROCEDURAL PLAN

A procedural plan is a uniform, systematic way of testing your hypothesis. Such testing requires that you first correlate what you want to prove. Correlation is done with two or more variables—dependent and independent. The dependent variable is the one that is being measured; the independent variable is the one that is controlled or manipulated by the experimenter. For example, you may want to see whether the health and growth of a tomato plant (the dependent variable) is influenced by the amount of light the plant is exposed to (the independent variable). Several other independent variables may be used instead, such as water, oxygen, carbon dioxide, nitrogen levels, etc. However, for the sake of clarity we will use only light for this example.

ESTABLISH A CONTROL GROUP

Next, an experimental group and a control group must be established. The control group provides you with a basis for comparing the experimental group. For example, your experimental group of tomato plants is placed in a sunny window for two weeks and watered periodically. At the end of the period, the plants have grown three inches and are very green. At this point, you may conclude that sunlight does indeed increase plant growth. But before you draw this conclusion, you should determine whether the tomato plants would grow and become green without any sunlight at all. This is where a control group of plants is needed.

The control group of plants would be those that are given the same treatment as the experimental ones, with the exception that they not be exposed to sunlight. If the outcome of the experiment showed that there was a significant difference between the two groups, then you probably would be justified in concluding that tomato plant growth is influenced by the amount of sunlight the plant receives.

The procedural plan in this example is very simple, but it gives you an idea of the process of an experiment. In essence, the procedural plan advances from one stage to another in an organized fashion. Remember, however, that most experiments are usually not as simple as the one described here. Often, obstacles arise and other interesting characteristics of the subject are revealed in the process. You may even discover existing differences in several trials with only one variable. In fact, this is a frequent occurrence, and it is an important reason why you must keep accurate data records.

ORGANIZE YOUR DATA

Data are essentially groups of figures for a given experiment. During the initial stages of an experiment, they may have little meaning, so it is important that you compile and organize your data accurately for your final analysis, observations, and conclusions. A good way to keep data is to record them in your project journal. After you have written down all the experimental results in an organized way, you can easily refer to your results to make generalizations and conclusions. There are several methods of presenting data, including the basic tabular, graphic, and statistical methods.

21

PRESENT YOUR DATA

Tabulating and Graphing

As mentioned above, raw data have little or no meaning in and of themselves. It is only when they are organized into tabular and graphic forms that they can be understood in terms of a scientific method or objective. The data results must be grasped quickly and correctly by the observer, so that he or she can see the project in a coherent perspective. Tables are relatively simple to make and form the basis for most graphs. The main points to consider are organization and coordination. For example, consider these recordings in tabular form of the body temperature of a flu patient:

Times	Body Temperature °F
6:00 A.M.	97.0
8:00 A.M.	98.0
10:00 A.M.	99.0
12:00 Noon	100.0
2:00 P.M.	101.0
4:00 P.M.	102.0
6:00 P.M.	103.0
8:00 P.M.	102.0
10:00 P.M.	100.0
12:00 Midnight	98.0

If you want to see how the patient's temperature fluctuated during the day, you can do this by looking at the table. But if you wanted to see at a glance how the patient's temperature changed, a graphic representation would be more effective.

A line graph may be used for this analysis. A line graph is comprised of two axes; the *x*, or horizontal, and the *y*, or vertical. The *x* axis contains all the points for one set of data, and the *y* axis contains all the points for the other set of data.

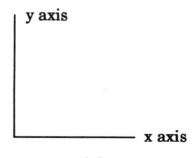

For example, you could label a range of body temperatures on the y axis and label the times on the x axis. After your axes are labeled, simply plot the points. Plotting involves matching each temperature with each corresponding time and marking them on the graph. For example, at 6:00 A.M. the body temperature was 97 degrees Fahrenheit, so you should locate and mark the point on the x and y axes at which 6:00 A.M. and 97 degrees correspond. Then do this for the rest of the data and connect the dots to complete the curve.

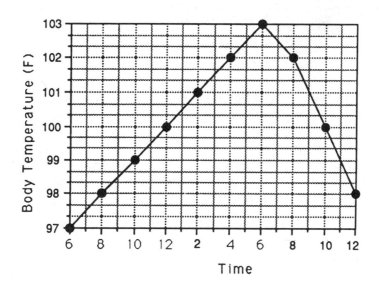

From this graph, one can quickly see that the patient's body temperature rose gradually, peaked late in the day, and fell during the evening. Another means of graphical representation that makes data easily understandable is the pie chart.

Suppose that you are testing a specimen of blood to determine the percentage of its composition of erythrocytes, leukocytes, and thrombocytes. After several tests and microscopical observation you conclude that the blood contained the percentages as shown in the following table:

Cell-type	% Composition
erythrocytes	50.0%
thrombocytes	38.0%
leukocytes	12.0%
$\Sigma^* =$	100.0%

*Σ is a Greek symbol that means "the summation of." The data listed above can be represented in a pie chart:

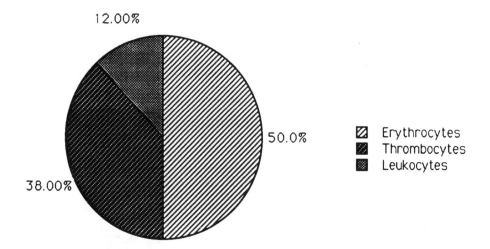

12.00%

50.0%

38.00%

Erythrocytes
Thrombocytes
Leukocytes

Each section represents a percentage of the pie. It is easy to see that the leukocyte blood count is low in terms of its percentage of the total composition.

There are many other ways to graph your data besides the two methods shown above. The important thing to remember about graphing is that it summarizes your results in a visual form that emphasizes the differences between groups of data results. As the old saying goes, a picture is worth a thousand words.

The Statistical Method

Some very simple statistics will allow you to expand on your data. Some of these applications include: the *mean, frequency distribution,* and *percentile.*

The **mean,** expressed as $\bar{x}$, where x is any rational number, is a mathematical average that is really the central location of your data. The sum of your data numbers is denoted by the symbol (Σ), which means, "the summation of." This sum is then divided by the quantity of your data recordings, which is the symbol (n). Thus, the mean is expressed as this formula:

$$\bar{x} = \frac{\Sigma x}{n}$$

For example, consider the mean fluoride level in parts per million from eleven different water departments.

Town Name	Fluoride Level (ppm*)
A-Town	1.00
B-Town	1.50

24

C-Town	1.50
D-Town	0.05
E-Town	0.04
F-Town	1.01
G-Town	0.09
H-Town	0.05
I-Town	2.00
J-Town	1.00
K-Town	1.00

$$\Sigma(x) = 9.24$$

*ppm means "parts per million"

Using the formula, you can express your results as follows: If $\Sigma(x) = 9.24$ and $n = 11$, then $\bar{x} = 9.24/11 = .8400$. The figure .8400 is the mean, or the mathematical average of the studied water plants.

Now suppose that you collected samples from fifty water plants. It may be difficult to generalize about the results, so a better method is needed to record the data. One way of describing the results statistically is by means of a **frequency distribution.** This method is a summary of a set of observations showing the number of items in several categories. For example, suppose that the following levels were observed to be present in fifty samples:

Fluoride Levels (ppm)	Frequency (f)
2.00	3
1.70	6
1.50	7
1.00	8
.90	10
.80	7
.05	6
.04	3
	$\Sigma f = 50n$

These results can be graphed using a histogram which represents your frequency distribution. With a histogram, your item classes are placed along the horizontal axis and your frequencies along the vertical axis. Then, rectangles are drawn with the item classes as the bases and frequencies as the sides. This type of diagram is useful because it clearly shows that the fluoride levels are normally at the .90 to 1.00 ppm mark.

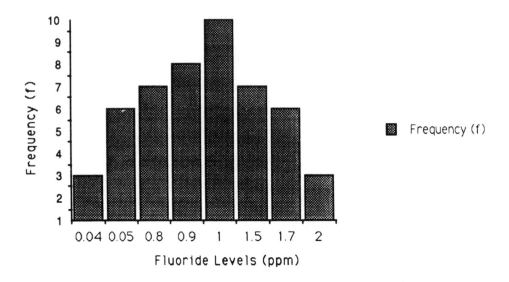

The **percentile** is another useful statistic. A percentile is the position of one value from a set of data that expresses the percentage of the other data that lie below this value. To calculate the value of a particular percentile, divide the percentile you want to find by 100 and multiply by the number of values in the ascending data set. If the answer is not an integer (a positive or negative whole number), round up to the next data value for the final answer. If the answer is an integer, average that number and the next data value for your answer. For example, suppose that you wanted to test the efficiency of 11 automobiles by measuring how many miles each car gets to a gallon of gasoline. You have recorded the following data: 17.6, 16.4, 18.6, 16.1, 16.3, 15.9, 18.9, 19.7, 19.1, 20.2, and 19.5. First, you would arrange the numbers in ascending order: 15.9, 16.1, 16.3, 16.4, 17.6, 18.6, 18.9, 19.1, 19.5, 19.7, and 20.2. Now suppose that you want to determine which car ranked in the 90th percentile. To calculate the 90th percentile for this data set, write this equation: $(90/100)(11)=9.9$. Since 9.9 is not an integer, round up to the tenth value for your answer. The tenth value is 19.7, therefore, the car that traveled 19.7 miles per gallon of gasoline is in the 90th percentile, and is one of the most gas-efficient cars in your study.

In summary, you will have to decide which tabular and graphical technique works best for your type of data. You can usually express your results in terms of either standard mathematical or statistical graphing. However, there are occasions when only one type will work. If you are dealing with numerous figures or classes of figures, a statistical graph usually works best. For example, if you wanted to demonstrate the variation of test scores between boys and girls in the eighth grade, you would probably make your point clearer by using the statistical method, which would allow you to find the percentiles in which each student

26

scored and the mean test score. On the other hand, if you were investigating the mineral composition of water, the best way to represent the proportion of its contents would be through a pie chart.

HOW TO AVOID A FAILED EXPERIMENT

There are several reasons why an experiment may fail to validate a hypothesis, prove a point, or simply do what it was intended to do. Such reasons include: mistakes in the way the experiment was carried out (procedural errors), a poor or incomplete final analysis, or erroneous hypotheses.

Procedural Errors

To avoid procedural problems, you must perform regular and consistent maintenance on your subject and controls. For example, in the experiment involving sunlight and tomato plants, if you gave the experimental group of tomato plants more water than the control group, or planted them in a soil that contained more nitrogen, you will get artificial results. This means that you are failing to control or hold your variable constant. How can you determine whether it was the sunlight alone or the combination of other factors that made the experimental tomatoes flourish? The same problem with inconsistent maintenance of controls might apply if you were studying the behavior of your friends at a party for a psychological experiment. What would happen if you made your study obvious by taking notes and pictures? Your friends probably would be influenced by your behavior and would not act in their usual manner. These examples involve manipulated experiments that would yield useless data. Of course, there are other procedural problems that arise during an experiment, especially if poorly calibrated measuring instruments are used.

Poor Final Analysis

Even after a carefully controlled experiment is completed, errors can still occur. Such errors could result from an incorrect analysis of results. For example, if you concluded that a certain salve cures acne, on the basis of tests that were conducted on female adolescents but not male ones, your final analysis would be inconclusive. While the salve may have worked on the females you tested, it may not work on females in different age groups, or on males of all age groups. Other problems with final analysis may arise from mathematical errors or from data that are irrelevant to the topic.

Erroneous Hypotheses

When an experiment is completed, the results are sometimes quite different from those that were predicted. If this occurs, do not manipulate the results to fit the initial hypothesis. Often, it may be that the hypothesis was incorrect or vague, and that the experimental results were accurate. If such problems occur in your project, you can salvage your work by finding out why the results were different than expected, or by explaining a new or unexpected observation or solution. This will show the judges that you remained interested and involved in the subject matter.

Keep in mind that many scientific investigations do not support their specific goals. However, this does not weaken the validity of their conclusions. In fact, many experiments require additional testing and exploration to understand a particular phenomenon. Sometimes, unexpected experimental results lead to surprising discoveries and more interesting science projects!

SUMMARY

1. The experiment is an essential part of your science project. It should test, survey, compare, and ultimately examine the validity of your hypothesis.
2. You must focus your topic on an experimental approach that will clearly test your hypothesis.
3. After you decide on an experimental approach, you must organize a procedural plan.
4. A procedural plan is a uniform, systematic way of testing a subject.
5. Data are recorded information that are organized for final analysis and observation.
6. The basic tabular, basic graphic, and statistical methods are ways of presenting data.
7. Three common ways in which an experiment can fail are: procedural errors, poor final analysis, and erroneous hypotheses.

Chapter 5

The Display

The display is an essential part of your project. Although it alone will not save a bad project, it can enhance the success of a good one. There is nothing more disappointing than to have a judge or viewer overlook a meritable project purely on the basis of its illegible or disorganized display. Therefore it is worth spending some extra time making an attractive display.

Your display should consist of a backboard, a report, and some tangible representation of your project, whether this includes the actual items used or studied, photographs, or simulated models.

An attractive display can enhance a project's success.

The information on your backboard should be placed in an orderly fashion from left to right under organized headings.

Your exhibit should display all aspects of your project. There are many ways to do this, but you must remember that all information should be self-explanatory. Lengthy discussions should be confined to the report.

THE BACKBOARD

The backboard probably will be the most important part of your display. It should include all the major parts of your project. The backboard is essentially an upright, self-supporting board with organized highlights of your project. It is usually three-sided, although it does not necessarily have to be. The backboard must meet the same spacing standards that are required for the International Science and Engineering Fair. The dimensions of your project must not exceed 9 feet in height, 30 inches in depth and 48 inches in width. If these dimensions are exceeded, you may be disqualified.

When constructing your backboard, it is a good idea to stay away from posterboard or cardboard. Backboards made of these materials tend to bend, and do not look very professional. It may be worth your while to purchase a firm, self-supporting material such as corkboard, pegboard, or wood panelling. In the long run, you will find these types of materials easier to work with and more attractive.

Select an appropriate lettering for your backboard. You might even want to purchase self-sticking letters, or make use of the services of a professional printer. In recent years, many students have produced attractive backboard lettering with a word processor. These machines are excellent tools that can move words in a piece of text, correct spelling errors, enlarge and reduce type, and create different lettering styles. Because there are so many lettering options available today, there is little reason to handprint your backboard.

Now that you know how to construct a backboard, you need to know what information you should put on it and where to place it. There is no standard way of making a backboard. However, all the information displayed on it should be well organized. The project title, for example, should stand out in the middle section in bold print. The rest of your information should be placed in an orderly fashion from left to right under organized headings. Some students even like to use the steps of the scientific method as their headings. Others apply headings that relate more specifically to their subject. Whatever headings you choose, make sure they are explicit and follow a format. After you plan out your format you can fill in extra spaces with additional information on your subject, such as photos, diagrams, and charts of various data.

The information that you place under each heading is crucial. It must be concise and inclusive. Do not fill up your backboard with excess information. Try to summarize the facts under each heading to no more than 300 words.

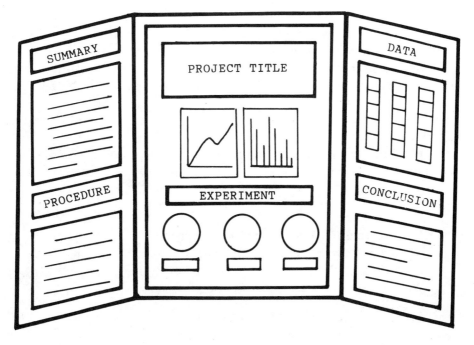

THE REPORT

It is also important that your report be of good quality. This means that you must organize a portfolio of clearly stated, factual information. It is important to keep this in mind because the report is essentially your spokesperson when you are not with your project.

An organized report contains the historical background on your subject, an introduction that states your purpose, a procedure that explains your means of acquiring information, your plan for organizing an experiment, and all the recorded data, diagrams, photos, conclusions, and other details that fully explain your project. You might even want to include detailed descriptions about different phases in your experiment in the form of a diary. It is a good idea to include the names and places you have visited, together with any related correspondence.

Your report may in fact be easier to complete if you create a journal (see Chapter 3). If you record everything as you go along, all you will need to do later is organize your notes, because your journal is essentially your report.

In organizing your report, you will have to distinguish between primary and secondary sources of information. Primary sources of information are those that consist of surveys, observations, and experimentations that you have done. Secondary sources are those types of information that have been obtained through outside sources, such as the library, media organizations, government agencies, and companies. When using secondary sources of information, you must acknowledge the source of any information taken directly or in part in footnotes and in a bibliography.

Be sure to type or print the final draft of your report. Remember, a report will not be able to explain your project as well as you can, but it is reassuring to know that an organized and professional report can work well for you in your absence.

You should also remember that if you write a thorough report that encompasses all the items mentioned here, you may also be eligible to submit it to another type of science competition, such as the Westinghouse Science Talent Search, or a local Junior Science and Humanities Symposium.

For more information on these types of competitions you may write or call:

The Westinghouse Science Talent Search
c/o Science Service
1719 N St., N.W.
Washington, D.C. 20036
202 785–2255

The National Junior Science and Humanities Symposium
98 Washington St.
Concord, NH 03301
603 228-4520
Doris Ellis, Director

THE ABSTRACT

An abstract is a brief summary of your project about 250 words in length. The abstract explains the project's purpose and procedural plan, and presents generalized data and a short discussion of your conclusions. There is no standard way to write an abstract, but it should always be brief and well written.

Some science fairs require that their finalists submit an abstract on judging day. A useful thing to do is to write your abstract in advance in order to avoid leaving out any necessary information. Even though the abstract does not affect your score or influence your final status, it is usually kept on record by your state science fair for future reference, and it may even be read by a special award sponsor.

DISPLAY RESTRICTIONS

You have read about the project limitation guidelines that are established by the International Science and Engineering Fair (ISEF). The ISEF also establishes strict regulations that involve the exhibition of certain items. Items that are prohibited include: live or preserved animals or their bodily parts, human parts, live disease-causing organisms, microbial cultures and fungi, food syringes, pipettes, hypodermic needles (or similar apparatus), drugs, dangerous chemicals, highly flammable or combustible materials, radioactive materials, batteries with open top cells, and the operation of Class III or IV lasers.

Certain items that are not restricted require special attention. Projects that involve wiring, switches, and metal parts that carry 110-volt power or higher voltage—such as radios and electronic devices—must be located out of reach of observers and be properly shielded to prevent accidents. Open knife switches and bare wire may be used only on circuits of 12 volts or less; otherwise standard enclosed switches are required. Sometimes, the best guide when considering safety issues is common sense and good judgment. For example, consider the possible consequences of displaying a petri dish of B-hemolytic streptococcus (the bacteria that causes strep throat), or of displaying an exposed laser beam with curious youngsters around. A rule of thumb is to avoid anything that could be potentially hazardous to display in public.

You can usually uphold such regulations by using photographs and model simulations. As always, however, if you have any doubts about displaying any part of your subject, be sure to first check with officials from your local science fair.

SUMMARY

1. The display of your science project must be presented in an organized and attractive manner.

2. The display consists of a backboard, a report, and a tangible representation of your project.

3. The ISEF has established regulations for the restriction and modification of potentially hazardous items.

4. Backboards must meet the standard space requirements established by the ISEF, which are 9 feet high, 30 inches deep, and 48 inches wide.

5. The report can be created primarily from a journal, but it must be organized around primary and secondary sources of information.

6. The abstract is a short essay that summarizes the goals, methods and conclusions of your project.

Chapter 6

At the Fair

The deadlines for the science fair approach faster than you may realize. This chapter should prepare you for what lies ahead. If you follow the format for completing a project that is recommended here, you should be successful. All that you need to be concerned with at this time is reserving a spot for your project and registering in the correct category.

At some state and regional fairs there are only two broad categories in which you may register—**biological sciences** and **physical sciences** (although there are several divisions within each of these categories that are designated by grade levels). The biological sciences category consists of projects that pertain to the life sciences, including behavioral sciences, biochemistry, botany, ecology, genetics, medicine and health, microbiology, zoology, animal species studies, disease studies, etc. The physical sciences category consists of projects that encompass chemistry, math, earth sciences, space science, engineering, physics, toxic waste studies, electronics, etc.

It is usually easy to determine where your project belongs, but sometimes it may be difficult. For example, if you did a project on prosthetic devices, in which you studied the physics of how artificial joints wear after a period of time, in what category would your project belong? If your project emphasized the amount of friction in the joint, it would probably be a physical project. But, if you began to discuss the biodegradability of the device, your project might be more appropriately placed in the biological category. The wrong choice could hurt your outcome in the competition.

As you set up your project, pay careful attention to the space requirements mentioned earlier (the space is usually marked off). Your backboard and display should already be self-supporting, but it is wise to bring tools such as a screwdriver, hammer, extension cord, stapler, glue, and tape in case your project needs minor repairs or modifications.

Your backboard should be self-supporting, but it is wise to bring glue, tape, and a stapler for minor repairs.

After your project is completely set up, a fair representative will check it to make sure everything complies with the fair rules and safety regulations. Make sure that you have everything displayed properly and have any necessary instructions available for the fair staff or judges (this is especially important if you have a project that involves the use of a computer or some other type of mechanically operated display).

JUDGING

Preliminary judging takes place after all the projects are set up. Students and parents are not allowed in the exhibit hall during this time. Generally, judges are assigned to separate divisions as teams. They begin by reviewing the projects in their category individually and then as a group, in which they exchange thoughts with team members and rank the projects.

The judges usually rank the projects by separating them into groups. For example, the Connecticut Science Fair groups its projects as follows: third honors (lower 50%), second honors (upper 50%), and first honors/finalist (top 10–15%). The third honors projects are determined first. The second honors and finalists are determined from the remaining projects. Only those projects that are finalists continue to compete for places in the overall competition. These finalists are notified by the fair and asked to be present for final judging on the following day.

State science fair finalists are asked to give several oral presentations for various judges. These judges may represent the fair itself, professional or academic organizations, or businesses that distribute specialized awards. Regular state science fair judges score the finalists on these six areas:

Scientific Thought/Engineering Goals (30 pts.). This area measures whether a project shows evidence of an applied scientific or engineering development through cause and effect, verification of laws, applied techniques for efficiency, or presentation of a new concept.

Creative Ability (30 pts.). This portion measures the ingenuity and originality in your approach to your topic.

Thoroughness (10 pts.). This area measures the variety and depth of the literature used, experimental investigation, and all other aspects of your project.

Skill (10 pts.). This aspect grades you on how much scientific and engineering practice you employed in your project. The level of experimentation, preparation, and treatment play an important role here.

Clarity (10 pts.). The exhibit should be presented in a way that is easily understood. Judges measure whether you have created a careful, systematic layout of selected information with neat, legible type.

Finalists are asked to give several presentations for both fair judges and special award sponsors from different organizations and businesses.

Dramatic Value (10 pts.). Judges also grade you on whether your project is presented in a way that attracts attention through the use of graphics and layouts and appears interesting to viewers.

Keep in mind that judging is a difficult task that requires the skill and expertise of a wide range of qualified professionals. The judges are analyzing the quality of work that has been done on a subject matter that involves probing, testing, and reasoning in a creative sense. They are not interested in plain library research, meaningless collections, or copied text material.

Presenting Your Project in an Interview

By having the opportunity to be present with your project during the final stages of judging, you are placed in an enviable position. You will be able to explain in detail certain procedures and conclusions in your project. It is important to be concise and businesslike during this process. Give a meaningful summary of your work in an interview. Practice what you want to say first, before the fair, so that your presentation will be smooth and relaxed.

If a judge asks you a question for which you do not have an answer, explain that you have not come across that aspect in your research, but that you would be glad to inform the judges about another stage or area about which you are more knowledgeable. Do not say, "I don't know." Above all, do not make up a false explanation. The judge is obviously

Finalists should be sharp and strive to communicate accurately and thoroughly with judges.

38

capable of detecting any errors or fudged experimental results. Also, remember that the judge might already have seen a project similar to yours at a previous science fair.

Judging usually takes a few hours, so try to be consistent with every interviewer. Try to stay alert and concentrate on what you want to say. If you must leave your project momentarily, leave a note stating that you will return soon. General tips you should keep in mind for successful presentation are: know your material, be confident, communicate well, and be thorough.

SPECIALIZED AWARDS

There are also special areas of competition that are separate from the general fair honors. These special categories are accessible to those students who complete a project concentrated in a particular area of science. Besides being eligible for a regular award, these students may receive awards in the areas of mathematics, computer science, or energy and environmental sciences. Other specialized awards are presented by various companies and societies. These groups honor excellence in a subject area related to the particular field that their organization specializes in.

After final judging, scores are tallied, and the winners in each division are announced. The top high-school projects of an affiliated state or regional fair qualify for competition in the International Science and Engineering Fair. Simply making it to the state or regional fair is an honor, but only a few can experience the thrill of participating in the International Science and Engineering Fair.

INTERNATIONAL SCIENCE
AND ENGINEERING FAIR

The ISEF is the grand finale of all state and regional fairs in the United States and some foreign science fairs. The top high school students in each ISEF-affiliated fair can compete at this fair, which is held annually at a major city, usually in the United States. The fair has an average of about 600 to 700 contestants, who account for more than 350 affiliated fairs. To see if your state or regional science fair is an affiliated fair, see Appendix C.

The procedures at the ISEF are slightly different than those of its affiliates. Students may select one of thirteen categories in which to enter a project. Judging is essentially the same as in all the state and regional fairs, with the exception that it takes place on only one day. The contestants begin their day with interviews by a panel of judges. If they do well, they proceed into another round of judging. If they qualify again, they proceed to the third and final rounds, in which category winners are selected.

The ISEF is organized by Science Service, a national, nonprofit group. If you would like more information about science fairs and other science competitions in your area, you can write to:

Science Service
1719 N St., N.W.
Washington, D.C. 20036

CLOSING NOTES

Now it's time for you to get into the "driver's seat" and take off. But before you get started, congratulate yourself for beginning your scientific career and for taking the time to thoroughly prepare for participation in a science fair.

This book was written to alleviate the frustration that often arises when students begin their first science project. It attempts to explain the strategies and shortcuts often used by finalists. Although the book cannot guarantee that you will make it to the top with your first science project, it can help you to prepare for science fairs and increase your motivation for future successes with science projects. Chances are good that your achievement will be recognized by college and business recruiters, who are looking for scientific talent and dedication. Remember, many of today's respected scientists began their careers in researching and engineering by participating in science fairs. You can do so as well by investing time and talent in a science project. The dividends will be a great future!

SUMMARY

1. It is important that contestants check with state science fair officials to register on time and in the correct category and division.

2. You should remember the following points when completing your projects:
   a. Scientific thought/engineering goals
   b. Creative ability
   c. Thoroughness
   d. Skill
   e. Clarity
   f. Dramatic value

3. Finalists should be concise and businesslike during the judging process and should strive to communicate with honesty and thoroughness.

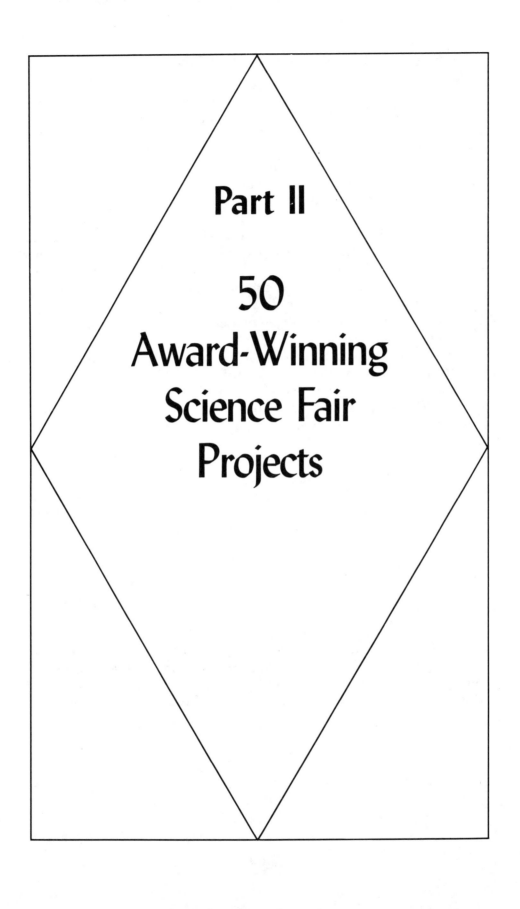

Part II

50
Award-Winning
Science Fair
Projects

IMPORTANT NOTES BEFORE YOU BEGIN

The following pages contain outline samples for 50 award-winning science fair projects. The summaries and diagrams should help you to prepare your project, particularly if you are a first-time science fair participant. These outlines are not intended to do the work for you, but to provide you with a variety of useful models to follow. The results of these 50 projects have thus been eliminated, and lists of questions have been prepared instead, so that you may have a guide for drawing conclusions about the projects.

The summaries of four International Science and Engineering Fair projects are also included in order to give you a sense of the caliber that is required for this highest level of competition. You will also see that one of the international projects appears again in a different form. This second experiment is included so you can see how successful science fair projects can be further researched and developed into even more successful projects.

As you read through these projects, you may require information about where to obtain some of the scientific equipment mentioned in the experiments. Refer to Appendix B for a list of scientific supply companies from which laboratory equipment and other supplies may be purchased. Also, some experiments list metric units of measure that may be unfamiliar to you or may require conversion to conventional units of measure. Refer to the metric conversion table at the beginning of the book for information about converting measurements.

Finally, you should keep in mind that the project outlines come from a variety of scientific disciplines and require minimal to advanced levels of scientific skill. The outlines come from award-winning projects on different grade levels. Therefore, while students with little science experience may find the international or engineering projects difficult, they should find others particularly suitable. Where noted, the assistance of a research scientist is required, precautions must be taken, and special skills are needed for certain projects. Be sure to heed these notices. They are there for your safety and to let you know whether or not a particular project is for you. In addition, check with your science fair project advisor first before starting any project appearing in this book for further guidance and safety precautions. Most importantly, exercise common sense and good judgment when conducting any science experiment.

Which Characteristic Is Most Influential in Attracting Bees to a Flower: Fragrance, Color, or Flavor?

PURPOSE

To determine the color, fragrance, and flavor that are most attractive to bees. Then, to determine which of these three characteristics plays the most important role in attracting bees.

MATERIALS NEEDED

Note: Protective clothing should be worn and caution exercised when approaching the beehive.

- 6 posterboards
- 9 assorted types of flowers
- food processor
- cheesecloth
- 8 oz. cup
- brush

- colored construction paper (9 different shades are necessary: white, red, orange, yellow, green, blue, violet, light pink, and dark pink)
- salt, sugar, lemon juice, and chokecherries (or a food with a similarly bitter taste)
- beehive

EXPERIMENT

The color, fragrance, and flavor variables will be isolated to identify the one that bees tend to go to first. For the fragrance test, several flowers that bees are known to pollinate will be pulverized individually in a food processor and strained through cheesecloth to collect the residue. The residue will then be streaked into separate circles on a posterboard. For

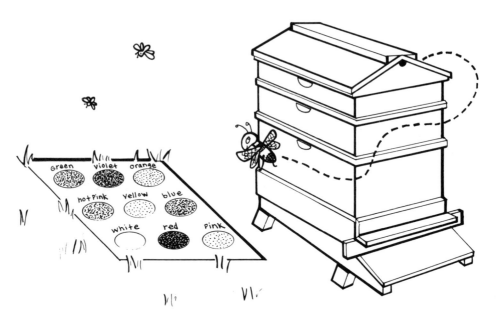

At first, each posterboard will be placed in front of the beehive to see which specific color, fragrance, and flavor are most attractive to the bees. Then, the three posters containing the separated variables only will be placed side by side to see which characteristic is most influential.

the color test, 5-inch diameter circles will be cut out of nine different shades of paper and glued onto another piece of posterboard. For the flavor test, various flavors will be smeared over another posterboard surface. Then, combinations of the three variables will be made. The bees' reactions and selections will be recorded.

PROCEDURE

1. Draw nine, 5-inch diameter circles in pencil on one of the poster-boards. Be sure to space them evenly on the board.

2. Obtain nine types of flowers and cut them from their stems. Pulverize them individually in a food processor. Then strain each pulverized flower through cheesecloth into the 8 oz. cup. With a brush, spread the residue from each flower in a separate circle on the posterboard. Be sure to label the type of flower each smear came from.

3. Cut nine, 5-inch diameter circles out of different colored construction paper: white, red, orange, yellow, green, blue, violet, light pink, and dark pink. Space them randomly on another piece of posterboard and glue them in place.

4. Take samples of the four basic food tastes (sweet, sour, salty, and bitter) from the sugar, lemon juice, table salt, and chokecherries, and

spread them separately on the third posterboard. Be sure to label them.

5. For the remaining three posterboards, create the following combinations of characteristics: place each flower fragrance on a separate colored circle, place each flavor on a separate colored circle, and finally, mix the flavors with the various flower fragrances. Be sure to label them.

6. Begin your experiment with the first posterboard of fragrances. Place the board approximately six feet in front of a beehive and stand several feet further away. Note the fragrance to which the bees are consistently attracted. Remove the board and replace it with the board that contains only colors. Again, stand a few feet away and see what color most attracts the bees. Do the same with the flavor board to see which flavor the bees are drawn to. Record your observations.

7. Test to verify your results by trying the combination boards. For example, if the bees in Step 6 favored the color violet, a sweet flavor, and the fragrance of lilacs, see if those results hold true when the violet circle is covered with either the sugar or lilac residue.

8. Test to see which of the three characteristics is the most influential in attracting the bees by placing all three posterboards from Step 6 side by side in front of the hive. Note the board that most consistently attracts the bees.

RESULTS

1. Were all of the bees consistent in their preferences?
2. What color, fragrance, and flavor seemed to most attract the bees?
3. Did the bees tend to favor the same color when it was combined with different fragrances and flavors? Did the same hold true for the fragrance and flavor variables?
4. Of all the colors, fragrances, and flavors, which single characteristic appeared to be the most influential in attracting bees?

2

The Effects of Gender Identity on Short-Term Memory

PURPOSE

To graph and compare the effects of gender identity on the short-term memories of varying age groups of children.

MATERIALS NEEDED

◆ 50 human subjects:
5 boys and 5 girls in the 1st grade
5 boys and 5 girls in the 2nd grade
5 boys and 5 girls in the 3rd grade
5 boys and 5 girls in the 4th grade

5 boys and 5 girls in the 5th grade

◆ grid containing 20 simple black-and-white pictures traditionally gender-typed for males (for example, a football) and for females (for example, a doll), arranged in alternate positions.

◆ stopwatch

EXPERIMENT

Each subject will be given 15 seconds to study the grid pictures. When the grid is taken away, the subject will be asked to list the names of the objects he or she can recall. It is believed that children will recall objects traditionally associated with their own gender.

PROCEDURE

1. Test five boys and girls from each grade individually. Test each subject in a quiet room that is free of distractions. Read the following

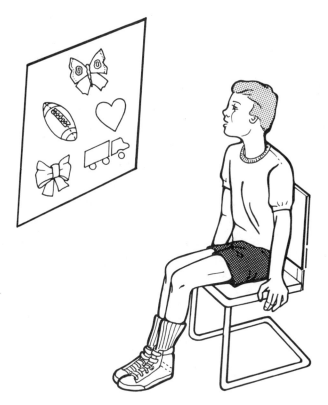

Each child will be given 15 seconds to study
traditionally gender-typed grid pictures. When the grid
is taken away, the subject will be asked to list the
names of the objects he or she can recall.

directions to each participant: "I will show you some pictures for
15 seconds. When the time is up, I will take the pictures away and
ask you to list the names of as many pictures as you can remember."

2. Tabulate the results using two different methods of analysis.

First Analysis: Group your data according to whether each subject
remembers a majority or a minority of the items traditionally associated with his or her gender, or simply an equal number of both male
and female gender-typed pictures.

Second Analysis: Examine whether there is a tendency for either the
male or female subjects to be influenced by the gender-typing of
the pictures presented. Record the total number and percentage of
the male gender-typed pictures recalled by the subjects as a group,
and do the same with the female gender-typed pictures. Repeat for
each grade level.

RESULTS

1. Did the boys, as a whole group, recall a majority or a minority of male gender-typed pictures? Or, did they recall an equal number of male and female gender-typed pictures?

2. Did the girls, as a whole group, recall a majority or a minority of female gender-typed pictures? Or, did they recall an equal number of male and female gender-typed pictures?

3. When grouped by grade, did the boys recall male gender-typed pictures at a greater frequency than female gender-typed pictures?

4. When grouped by grade, did the girls recall female gender-typed pictures at a greater frequency than male gender-typed pictures?

5. Do the results change for each grade level? If so, what variables may have influenced the results of the varying grade levels? What are the implications of these results?

3

Do All Plants Transpire at the Same Rate Under Different Sources of Light?

PURPOSE

To determine if various species of plants transpire at the same rate under different sources of light.

MATERIALS NEEDED

- 12 2-liter plastic soda bottles
- potting soil (enough to fill 12 soda bottle bottoms)
- 3 jade plants
- 3 African violet plants
- 3 ivy plants
- 3 polka dot plants
- 3 cups water
- household lamp
- fluorescent lamp
- sunlight
- spatula
- graduated measuring cup

EXPERIMENT

Three plants of four different species will be placed in the removable bottoms of 12 plastic soda bottles. The removable tops of the soda bottles will be cut to fit within the soda bottle bottoms to form a kind of convertible terrarium. One sample of each plant species will be placed in the presence of all three different light sources: direct sunlight, a fluorescent lamp, and a household lamp, for a period of six hours. The amount of transpiration among the plants will then be compared and recorded.

PROCEDURE

1. Pull the plastic supporting bottoms from 12 2-liter soda bottles and fill them with potting soil. Then cut the rounded bases from the upper portions of the soda bottles and put them aside.

2. Obtain three young plants from each of four different species and transplant them into the 12 plastic soda bottle bottoms.

3. Water each plant with ¼ cup of water and fit the soda bottle tops over the plants to create a terrarium (this will allow you to trap and measure the amount of water that the plants transpire). Also, be sure to place labels on each bottle top to specify the type of plant and the light source to which it will be exposed.

4. Place each plant species in the presence of all three light sources for six hours.

5. After the light exposure, remove the upper portions of the soda bottles carefully so that the water that has transpired onto them will not roll off. Then remove the water from each container with a spatula and measure with the measuring cup the quantity of water that transpired from each plant.

6. Repeat Steps 4 and 5 several times to obtain more accurate results.

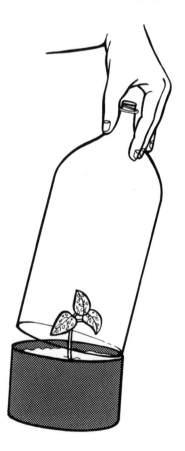

The plastic supporting bottoms will be removed from 12 2-liter soda bottles and used as pots for the various plants. Then, the rounded bases of the upper portions of the soda bottles will be cut to fit over the plants to form a terrarium.

RESULTS

1. What amounts of water did each plant transpire under the different light sources?

2. Did the same plant species transpire equal amounts of water under all three light sources?

3. Which light source induced the most transpiration?

4. What outside variables may have influenced your results?

4

Can Plant Cloning Be Used Effectively by Produce Growers?

PURPOSE

To try to make a more perfect carrot and green bean by cloning rather than using the traditional cultivating methods, which may yield a lesser quality vegetable or one that contains artificial chemicals and sprays. Also, to determine whether cloning is a faster and more effective means for farmers to grow crops.

MATERIALS NEEDED

- carrot seeds from an unblemished organically grown carrot
- green bean seeds (same as above)
- pots for plants
- vermiculite
- greenhouse incubator
- seed germination media

- measuring cup
- bunsen burner
- 30 petri dishes
- potting soil
- scalpel and forceps
- callus initiation media, 150 milliliters
- plastic bags
- clone induction media, 150 milliliters

EXPERIMENT

Both the carrot and green bean seeds will be planted in vermiculite (to serve as a control of a traditional cultivating method) and in the seed germination media that has been melted into some of the petri dishes. After this latter group has grown, it will be transferred to the callus initiation media followed by the clone induction media. The growth rates of the plants and the quality of their produce will be analyzed in comparison to the control plants and produce.

PROCEDURE

1. Plant some of the carrot and green bean seeds in vermiculite and put them into the greenhouse incubator. These will serve as the control group.

2. Melt the seed germination media in a cup over a bunsen burner and pour it into 10 petri dishes equally. When solid, drop some of the carrot and green bean seeds onto the surface of the petri dishes. Growth will show in two weeks. These will serve as the experimental group.

3. When the plants in the control group are at least 4 inches tall, uproot them and put them into pots of potting soil. When the experimental plants are also 4 inches tall, cut their roots and leaves off. Cut their remaining stems into 1 cm pieces. Melt the callus initiation media in a cup over a bunsen burner and pour equally into ten of the petri dishes. Next, place the stem sections onto the solidified petri dishes. Cover the dishes and put them into plastic bags.

4. Within a month, shoots will be visible. At this time, melt some of the clone induction media and pour it into the remaining 10 petri dishes. Using a scalpel, cut around the stem sections, including the callus initiation media. With forceps, place the cuttings on the solidified clone induction media. Cover the dishes and place them in the plastic bags again.

5. As soon as growth is detected on the petri dishes, add some soil to the dishes to help the growth along. After they have grown a few inches, plant each of them into pots. Continue to care for the plants and observe their overall health and growth and the quality of their produce.

RESULTS

1. Compare the growth of the seeds that were cultivated in the vermiculite and greenhouse incubator to those cultivated on the seed germination media. Which grew faster? Which looks healthier?

2. Did the carrot plant or the green bean plant grow quicker when it was cut and placed on the callus initiation media?

3. Did the final plant clones look healthy? Did the difference in their original growth area affect their outcome?

4. Were the vegetables that were produced from the cloned plants as attractive as their ancestors? Were they of a higher quality than those produced from the control (vermiculite) plants?

5

How Effective Is Beta Carotene in Fighting Cancer in Plants?

PURPOSE

To determine whether beta carotene has any substantial effect in reducing or eliminating the presence of *Agrobacterium tumefaciens.*

MATERIALS NEEDED

- packet of sunflower seeds
- all-purpose potting soil
- 3 flower pots
- tap water
- beta carotene (vitamin A) solution (5 caplets to 1 pint water)
- disinfectant
- inoculating needle
- candle or match
- *Agrobacterium tumefaciens* (a plant carcinogen)

EXPERIMENT

The sunflower seeds will be divided into three equal groups. Group A will be germinated in the beta carotene solution, while Groups B and C will be germinated in tap water only. After the seeds have germinated, they will be planted in all-purpose potting soil. Groups A and B will be given the carcinogen and will serve as the experimental groups, while Group C will be carcinogen-free and serve as the control. Group A will then be watered bi-weekly with the beta carotene solution. Groups B and C will be watered bi-weekly with tap water.

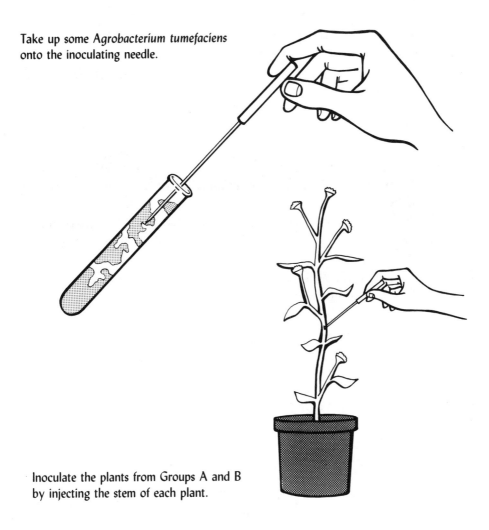

Take up some *Agrobacterium tumefaciens* onto the inoculating needle.

Inoculate the plants from Groups A and B by injecting the stem of each plant.

PROCEDURE

Divide the sunflower seeds into three groups. Germinate the seeds in Group A in the beta carotene solution, and the seeds in Groups B and C in tap water.

1. Allow all the plants to grow approximately 7–10 inches, after which the plants in Group A and Group B will be ready for innoculation. At this time, thoroughly clean the working area with a disinfectant.

2. Sterilize the innoculating needle by holding it for 3 seconds in the flame of a candle or match. Draw some of the *Agrobacterium tume-faciens* culture onto the needle tip and inject the plants from Group A. Then, sterilize the needle once again and innoculate the plants from Group B. Do not inoculate Group C, because it is the control group.

3. Continue to water the plants in Group A bi-weekly with the beta carotene solution and the plants in Groups B and C with tap water.

4. Record growth rates of the plants each week and note their appearance and rate of deterioration.

RESULTS

1. Compare the growth of the plants before the innoculation process. Rate the plants according to their amount of growth and general state of health.

2. Compare the growth of the plants after the innoculation process. Rate the plants according to their amount of growth and general state of health.

3. Do you believe that the beta carotene solution had any effect at all on reducing or eliminating the disease of Group A?

6

The Effect of Electromagnetic Fields on *Eremosphaera* Algae Cells

PURPOSE

To determine if and how electromagnetic fields affect the numbers and appearances of algae cells at increasingly higher levels.

MATERIALS NEEDED

- *Eremosphaera* algae colony
- dropper
- slides
- microscope
- 7 test tubes
- spring water
- electrical wire
- 2-light bath bar light fixture
- 2 Gro-light brand fluorescent bulbs
- wood panel (upright and self-supporting)
- hammer and nails
- thermometer

EXPERIMENT

The algae colony will be divided into seven equal groups and placed into seven test tubes filled with ⅛ cup of water. Groups 1–6 will be placed in the electromagnetic apparatus by being encircled by increasing levels of spiraled electrical wire. Group 7 will serve as the control and will not be exposed to the electromagnetic fields of the apparatus by being placed in another room. The algae will be left within their electromagnetic fields for a period of time and will then be analyzed.

PROCEDURE

1. Divide the *Eremosphaera* algae colony into seven equal groups. Observe a droplet specimen from each group on a slide under a microscope. Record the appearance of the cell structures and the amount of cells present. Transfer each group into a different test tube and fill each tube with ⅛ cup of spring water. Label each test tube 1–7.

2. Then, wrap one layer of five coils around test tube 1, three layers of five coils around test tube 2 (=15 spirals), six layers of five coils around test tube 3 (=30 spirals), nine layers of five coils around test tube 4 (=45 spirals), twelve layers of five coils around test tube 5 (=60 spirals), and fifteen layers of five coils around test tube 6 (=75 spirals). Test tube 7 will not be wrapped with electrical wiring (see diagram).

3. Allow for a 6-inch space between each test tube (with the exception of tube 7 which will be exposed to the normal electromagnetic fields found in another room of your house).

4. Carefully nail the back of the light fixture to an upright, self-supporting wood panel. Then plug the apparatus into a nearby wall outlet.

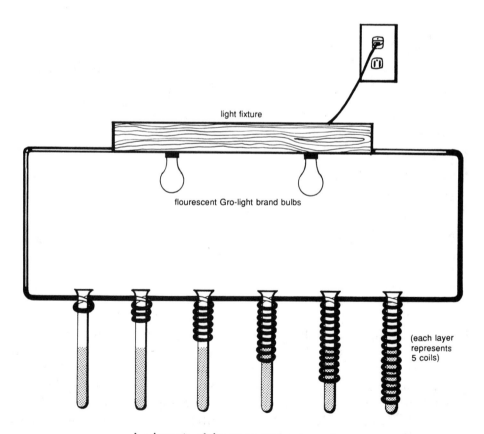

A schematic of the set-up testing apparatus.

5. Leave the tubes exposed for about an hour, turn off the power and measure the temperature within each vial. Then, take a droplet specimen from each tube again to record your observations of the cell structures and the number of cells.

RESULTS

1. Compare the appearance and number of cells found initially in each test tube to those found at the end of the experiment. Did they vary within the same tube?

2. Did the cell appearances and quantity change from tube to tube? Were these changes more apparent as higher electromagnetic fields were introduced?

3. Compare the temperatures of all the tubes. At higher temperatures what changes occurred?

What Is the Most Efficient Substance for Melting Ice?

PURPOSE

To determine the most effective of seven substances traditionally used for melting ice.

MATERIALS NEEDED

- 14 aluminum foil baking pans (8″ × 8″ × 2″)
- water to fill each pan
- 1 cup calcium chloride
- 1 cup of a commercial brand of melting crystals
- 1 cup sodium chloride
- 1 cup cat box litter
- 1 cup sand

- 1 cup rubbing alcohol
- 1 cup mineral rock salt
- large freezer (experiment can be done outside if temperature is below 32° Fahrenheit)

EXPERIMENT

Fourteen aluminum foil baking pans containing ice will be subjected to equivalent amounts of different substances commonly used to melt ice. Each pan will be individually timed so as to determine which substance, and the way it is applied, will be the most effective in melting the ice. Comparisons will then be made between each substance to see the amounts of residue each has left and whether that residue could have damaging effects on paved driveways and sidewalks.

PROCEDURE

1. Fill seven aluminum baking pans with water and freeze them either in a large freezer or outdoors. Label this lot Group A.

2. Pour $\frac{1}{2}$ cup of each of the seven substances separately into the remaining seven baking pans. Label each pan with the name of its corresponding substance. Carefully fill the pans with water and place them either in a large freezer or outdoors to freeze. Label this lot Group B.

3. When the water in Group A has completely solidified, pour $\frac{1}{2}$ cup of each substance into separate pans in Group A. Label each pan with the name of its corresponding substance.

4. At this point, all 14 pans of ice will be in contact with one of the substances. Measure the melting time of each pan in Group A in half-hour intervals. Note the progress of the melting process over a three-hour period and record your results. Check on Group B in half-hour intervals also, to note the rate of any ice formation over a three-hour period. Record your results.

5. Pour the contents of each baking pan in Group A into separate sections of a paved driveway and label. Pour the contents of Group B into separate sections of a cement sidewalk and label. Allow all of the water to evaporate. Let the different types of residue stay where they are for 4–6 weeks. After this time, sweep them away and note any damage that has resulted. Compare the effects of the same substances on both surfaces.

RESULTS

1. Which substance in Group A melted the ice the fastest? How well did this substance prevent the formation of ice in Group B?

2. Did the addition of the ice-melting substances prior to the application of water in Group B slow or prevent the formation of ice? Does this mean that such substances should be applied to driveways and sidewalks when precipitation and frigid temperatures are expected?

3. Did any of the substances' residue cause damage to either the paved driveway or the sidewalk? If so, what type of damage did you observe?

4. In terms of speed, efficiency, and cost, which substance was the best?

8

What pH Level Is Most Conducive to Corrosion in Iron and Copper?

PURPOSE

To determine the pH level that induces the most corrosion in the least amount of time on iron and copper in the presence of oxygen.

MATERIALS NEEDED

- 14 glass cups
- hydrochloric acid
- sodium hydroxide
- distilled water
- litmus paper

- 28 test tubes
- iron filings to fill 14 test tubes halfway
- copper filings to fill 14 test tubes halfway

EXPERIMENT

Fourteen test tubes will be half filled with iron filings and another fourteen will be half filled with copper filings. Each tube will then receive a successive amount of a pH-balanced solution of hydrochloric acid, sodium hydroxide, and distilled water. The tubes will be exposed to the various solutions for one month with the exception that they will be exposed to oxygen daily for 30 minutes. Each sample will be analyzed daily and at the end of the experiment to note its rate of oxidation.

PROCEDURE

1. Fill 14 cups with varying proportions of the hydrochloric acid, sodium hydroxide, and distilled water to achieve pH levels from 1 (acidic) to 14 (basic). Test with litmus paper to make sure you have

14 different pHs. (In an acid solution, the paper will turn bright red. In an alkaline solution, the paper will turn blue.)

2. Fill 14 test tubes halfway with the iron filings and mark the test tubes from 1–14a. Fill the second 14 test tubes with the copper filings and mark them from 1–14b.

3. Pour half of each pH solution into the iron filings and half into the copper filings. Each test tube should be about ¾ full.

4. Leave the filings inside their respective pH solutions for about 30 days. But, allow the filings to air out by scooping them out of their test tubes and laying them each on separate paper towels for 30 minutes each day. Observe and record the changes that take place in each test tube daily.

RESULTS

1. Which pH level induced the most corrosion in the iron filings? In the copper filings? Which pH level induced the fastest rate of corrosion on iron? On copper? How soon after the beginning of the experiment did you observe these changes?

2. Did the higher pH levels induce more corrosion than the lower pH levels?

3. Did the iron and the copper corrode in the same way?

4. Did any of the pH levels appear to inhibit corrosion?

9

How Effective Is Lobster Shell Chitin in Filtering Wastewater Metallic Ions?

PURPOSE

To test the filtration abilities of chitin, to compare it with charcoal, a common water filter, and to determine how chitin absorbs metals.

MATERIALS NEEDED

- 6 test beakers
- Standard Methods of Atomic Absorption (can be found in a chemistry book)
- metals (iron, lead, zinc, iridium, tin, and silver) and solvents for preparing 6 different 100 milligrams/liter metal solutions
- distilled water
- 12 squares of cheesecloth
- 12 rubber bands
- glass tube (hollow with two open ends)
- 300 grams chitin (obtained by cleaning, drying, and chopping lobster shells into ½ centimeter pieces) per metal solution
- ringstand and clamps
- funnel
- Atomic Absorption Instrument to measure a solution's metallic concentration
- 300 grams activated carbon (charcoal) per metal solution
- stopwatch

EXPERIMENT

Several solutions of metals and solvents will be filtered through chitin and charcoal. The filtration effectiveness of each will be compared by measuring the amount of time it takes for each solution to run through both filters, and by measuring the concentration of metallic ions present in the solutions' effluent after they have passed through both filters.

PROCEDURE

1. In six separate beakers, prepare a 100 mg/L solution for each of the types of metals, according to the Standard Methods for Atomic Absorption.

2. Fold a square of cheesecloth into four layers and secure it over one end of the glass tube with a rubber band. Place 50 g of the chitin into the other end of the tube. Then, attach the tube to the ringstand and place the funnel on the glass tube.

3. Remove 10 ml of one solution, measure its metallic concentration with the Atomic Absorption Instrument, and record it. This will be

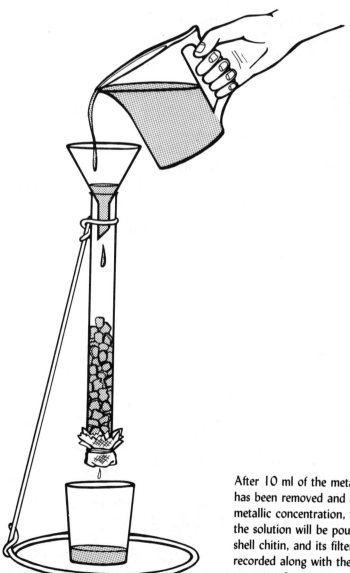

After 10 ml of the metallic/water solution has been removed and measured for its metallic concentration, the remainder of the solution will be poured through lobster shell chitin, and its filtering time will be recorded along with the effluent's metallic concentration.

the control. Pour the remaining solution through the apparatus and record the time it takes for the solution to run through the filter and collect as effluent into a cup. Then, test the effluent's metallic concentration with the Atomic Absorption Instrument and record it.

4. Repeat Steps 2 and 3 with other metallic solutions. Whenever a different solution is used, clean the tube and use new chitin and cheesecloth.

5. Then, repeat Steps 1–4, replacing the chitin with 50 g charcoal for each metallic solution.

RESULTS

1. Compare the concentrations of the solutions before and after filtration. What percentage of metal did the chitin remove from each solution? What percentage of metal did the charcoal remove from each solution?

2. Compare the filtration times of the chitin and the charcoal. Does the rate at which a solution passes through either filter affect its metallic concentration?

3. Which metals were absorbed best in the chitin? Check the oxidation states of the metallic ions in the solutions. Do you think that the oxidation states of the metals are due to their filtration through the chitin?

How Does Saltwater Mix in an Estuary?

PURPOSE

To determine the average and individual concentrations of salt from various points along an estuary by analyzing the color, density, and residue of the water.

MATERIALS NEEDED

- 2-liter samples estuary water from seven locations along an estuary
- 250 milliliter beaker
- 14 test tubes
- 4-liter sample fresh river water (or substitute distilled water)

- 4-liter sample saltwater
- graduated cylinder
- 15 plastic cups
- balance scale

EXPERIMENT

Three different tests will be used to analyze estuary water. The first test will focus on color variations to distinguish the salt water from the river water. The second will measure the density of the estuary water to determine the amount of sea water that has been mixed in. The third test will measure the residual percentage of salt after the water has evaporated.

PROCEDURE

*Test A—to determine visually the average amount of
saltwater present within samples from various locations
along an estuary.*

1. Boil the seven 2-liter samples of estuary water separately until each is reduced to 250 ml. Then fill seven test tubes halfway with each of the concentrated samples.

2. Next, make seven saltwater/fresh river water color samples with which to compare the concentrated estuary samples. Fill the first test tube halfway with 100% fresh river water, the second with 100% saltwater, the third with 80% fresh river water and 20% saltwater, the fourth with 60% fresh river water and 40% saltwater, the fifth with 50% fresh river water and 50% saltwater, the sixth with 40% fresh river water and 60% saltwater, and the seventh with 20% fresh river water and 80% saltwater.

3. Compare the colors of the samples of concentrated estuary water to the colors of the reference samples in the test tubes. For each estuary sample, record the reference sample that most closely resembles it in color.

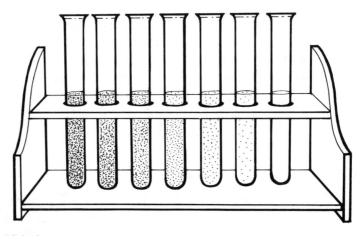

Saltwater and fresh river water color samples should be made with which to compare the concentrated estuary samples. Fresh river water is usually several shades browner than mixed fresh river water and seawater, while fresh seawater is usually clear.

*Test B—to determine the actual amount of saltwater mix
by calculating the densities of the seven samples.*

1. Using the graduated cylinder, measure 175 cc of each reference sample into a plastic cup and weigh them separately on a balance scale. Then subtract the cup's weight to obtain the mass of each sample.

2. Find the density of each sample by dividing the mass by the volume. Then calculate the average density for all the samples.

3. Next, find the actual percentage of saltwater for each sample. Once you have determined the separate and combined densities of the freshwater and saltwater in your sample and know the sample's total volume, the percentage of fresh river water (x) and saltwater (y) can be calculated as follows:

   [(volume of x)(density of x)] + [(volume of y)(density of y)] = total volume $\times$ density

*Test C—to measure the residual percentage of each
sample.*

1. Reduce 2 liters of an estuary location sample by boiling it. Allow it to cool and pour into a plastic cup. Place another cup alongside and fill it with distilled water until the volumes in both cups are the same.

2. Then weigh both cups on a balance scale and subtract the mass of the distilled water from the mass of the sample water. Repeat for each of the samples and record your results.

RESULTS

1. What were the levels of salt concentration among the samples? Were your color reference samples accurate as to the salt concentrations in each sample?

2. Were the results from each of the three tests consistent for each water sample?

3. Were the salinity levels consistent for all seven locations? If not, which location of the estuary had the highest level of salinity? The least?

4. Were you able to identify other minerals present in the samples?

5. Experiment with different estuaries. Are the salinity level distributions that you found in the original estuary comparable to those of other estuaries?

II

Can the Life Span of a Soap Bubble Be Extended in Different Temperatures and Atmospheric Conditions?

PURPOSE

To determine if certain substances can increase the life span of soap bubbles under varying temperature and atmospheric conditions.

MATERIALS NEEDED

- 3-quart glass, metal, or plastic container
- ½ cup dishwashing liquid
- water
- 9 plastic drinking straws
- thermometer
- stopwatch
- 8 clear glass jars with covers
- bubble additives:
  1 teaspoon school glue

3 drops food coloring
¼ teaspoon vanilla extract
¼ teaspoon witch hazel
¼ teaspoon olive oil
¼ teaspoon aftershave lotion
¼ teaspoon lemon juice

EXPERIMENT

Bernoulli's principle of raising and lowering a bubble due to its air pressure, will be tested with bubbles made from liquid soap under two types of atmospheric conditions: a hazy, hot, and humid environment, and a clear, cold environment. The same principle will be tested again with the soap bubbles mixed with bubble additives to see whether the bubbles will be altered in the same two environments. Finally, both types of bubbles will be blown into the eight glass jars, covered, and placed in a warm

70

room (80° Fahrenheit). The life span of each bubble will be timed until it pops. The same will be done in a cold room (45° Fahrenheit). Comparisons will be made between additives under differing temperature and atmospheric conditions.

PROCEDURE

1. On a clear, cold day, mix a solution of ½ cup dishwashing liquid with 2 quarts water in the container outdoors. Dip one end of a straw into the solution and blow from the other end to create a bubble. Shake the straw lightly to detach the bubble. With a stopwatch, time the life span of the bubble while testing Bernoulli's principle (wave your hand over the bubble to make it rise, then wave your hand under the bubble to make it sink). Repeat the same procedure

After the bubble additives have been mixed into seven of the eight jars, blow a bubble directly inside each jar and time its lifespan to see which substance holds a bubble the longest in a warm and in a cold environment.

on a hazy, hot, and humid day. Note any changes in the way the bubble forms and the length of time it remains intact.

2. Mix another solution of ½ cup dishwashing liquid and 2 quarts of water. Pour equal amounts of the solution into the eight jars. Add the specified amount of a different bubble additive to each jar, stir until dissolved, and label each jar. The eighth jar is the control and will contain soap bubbles only. Then, repeat Step 1 for the seven jars containing bubble additive only and record your results.

3. Bring all eight of the jars indoors. Using a different straw for each mixture, blow a bubble directly into each of the jars. Time the life span of each bubble. Cover the jars immediately and place them in a warm room heated to 80° Fahrenheit. Observe each bubble and record the time it takes for each to pop. Repeat this step in a room cooled to 45° Fahrenheit. You may also use a refrigerator.

RESULTS

1. Did the air pressure within the plain soapy bubbles change under different atmospheric conditions? If so, how did the bubbles react, and how long did they exist under each condition?

2. Did the bubble additives have any effect in changing the way the bubbles reacted to each environment? If so, what were these effects?

3. Do the plain soap bubbles or the bubbles with additives last longer under warmer or colder temperatures?

4. In which bubble additive solution did the bubbles last the longest under all conditions?

5. What practical applications might this experiment have for industry?

12

What Colored Dyes Are Found in Powdered Drink Mix and Colored Markers?

PURPOSE

To find out which colored dyes are used in powdered drink mix and in colored markers.

MATERIALS NEEDED

♦ ruler
♦ 20 paper coffee filters
♦ scissors
♦ dropper
♦ 10 packages of powdered drink mix, each of a different flavor

♦ water
♦ 10 small plates
♦ stapler
♦ 20 small glass jars with lids (or substitute plastic wrap)
♦ rubbing alcohol
♦ 10 differently colored felt tip markers

EXPERIMENT

Paper chromotography, which separates a mixture into its component pigments, will be used to analyze the various colored dyes present in 10 flavors of drink mix and 10 differently colored markers.

PROCEDURE

1. Cut a 19 cm × 19 cm rectangle from the bottoms of 20 paper coffee filters.
2. Make pencil marks 2 cm in from the longer sides of the cut-out rectangles. Draw a line connecting the marks.

A 19 cm × 19 cm rectangle, cut from the bottom of a coffee filter, with the drink mix or marker spot.

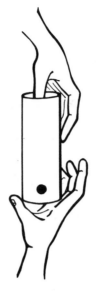

After the spot has dried, roll the filter paper into a cylinder and staple.

When the cylinder is placed in the center of the jar of rubbing alcohol for 15 to 20 minutes, the spot of drink mix or marker will separate into its component colors.

3. Mix a pinch of each flavor of powdered drink mix with a drop of water on each of the 10 small plates.

4. With the dropper place a droplet of each flavor on the pencil lines of 10 filters and allow them to dry. Label the names of each flavor in pencil.

5. When each paper has dried, staple each into a cylinder shape, with the droplet stain on the outside.

6. Fill the 10 jars about a centimeter high with rubbing alcohol.

7. Place one paper cylinder into each of the 10 jars without touching the sides of the jars.

8. Cover the jars with lids or plastic wrap.

9. Leave each paper cylinder in the alcohol for about 15 to 20 minutes, or until the alcohol reaches the top of the paper coffee filters.

10. Remove the paper filters, and allow them to dry. You have just made a chromotogram and should be able to see the different colored dyes that make up each of the 10 flavors used.

11. To experiment with the colored markers, repeat Steps 1–10, making colored marks on the paper filters instead of using the drink mix.

RESULTS

1. Were there more pigments in the chromotograms of the drink mix or the colored markers? What colors were visible in each chromotogram?

2. What pigments were found most often in the drink mix? What pigments were found most often in the colored markers?

3. Were the lighter colored drink mixes and markers made up of as many pigments as the darker ones?

4. Which of the component dyes traveled furthest up the filter paper? Why?

5. Were the drink mixes and colored markers of the same color made up of different pigments?

Can Ocean Waves Be Used to Generate Electricity?

PURPOSE

To find out how much power can be produced by a miniaturized ocean wave comprised of 2 gallons of water in order to determine whether a combination of such waves on a larger scale could serve as an alternative energy source.

MATERIALS NEEDED

- aquarium filter pump
- plastic tub (16″ × 25″ × 6″)
- rocks or bricks
- small generator with impeller (i.e., blade rotor) and voltmeter
- 2 gallons water

EXPERIMENT

A simulated ocean current will be produced by passing water through a narrow opening in a tub with an aquarium filter pump. The simulated current will then turn an impeller, which is attached to a generator with a voltmeter. The voltmeter will then determine how much electricity can be produced by 2 gallons of wave-driven water.

PROCEDURE

1. Attach an aquarium filter pump to one of the far ends of the tub (this will be considered the front of the tub).
2. Construct a narrow passageway along the length of the tub with rocks or bricks.

3. On the back end of the tub place a small generator with an attached impeller and voltmeter.

4. Fill the tub with 2 gallons of water and turn on the aquarium filter pump. The pumped water should then be forced through the narrow passageway into the back of the tub where the impeller should be rotated by the current.

5. Allow the waves to generate electricity for about a minute and then observe the amount of electricity that registers on the voltmeter.

RESULTS

1. How much electricity was produced by 2 gallons of water?

2. From this figure, hypothesize how much electricity could be produced by a given quantity of ocean water.

3. Was the aquarium filter pump the best device to use as a simulator of natural wave force? Do you think it may have presented some outside variables that need to be taken into account when calculating the amount of electricity actually produced?

14 Which Form of Insulation Is Most Effective?

PURPOSE

To test the effectiveness of various forms of insulation and to determine which would effectively retain the most heat and serve as the best insulator for warming the human body.

MATERIALS NEEDED

- 7 large plastic resealable sandwich bags
- equal portions of wool, flannel, human hair (can be obtained from a barbershop), thermal insulation, cotton, and chicken feathers (to pad plastic bags 2 cm thick all around)
- masking tape
- 7 pints water
- 7 1-pint canning jars with lids
- oven thermometer
- 7 regular thermometers
- refrigerator

EXPERIMENT

Seven water-filled jars will serve as a model of the human body. The plastic bags filled with insulating materials will represent the insulated clothing being tested.

PROCEDURE

1. Fill each plastic bag with one type of insulating material. Fasten the insulating materials to the bags with masking tape to equal 2 cm thick all around. Leave the seventh bag empty to serve as a control.

When the temperature reaches 70° Celsius in each jar, drop a regular thermometer into each jar and cap it quickly. Then, put each jar into a different insulator pouch.

2. Boil 7 pints of tap water and fill each of the seven canning jars with equal amounts of boiling water.

3. Immediately take the temperature of each jar with the oven thermometer and record it on a chart. When the temperature reaches 70° Celsius in each jar, drop a regular thermometer into each jar, and cap it tightly and quickly.

4. Put each jar into a different insulator pouch (including the empty pouch) and place in the refrigerator.

5. Keep the jars in the refrigerator for 2 hours. Take the temperature readings of each jar every 15 minutes and cap quickly after each reading. At the end of the 2 hours, compare readings and note how rapidly they changed over time relative to one another. Graph your data.

RESULTS

1. Was the jar in the control bag colder than the insulated jars?
2. Which insulator was most effective?
3. Which insulator was the easiest to work with and would be the most practical in winter clothing? What other insulators could be used in this experiment?

15

Alcohol as a Fuel: Recycling Wastes Into Energy

Enhan
E
M
S

PURPOSE

To see if it is possible for a household to construct a simple and inexpensive still capable of recycling its fermented organic garbage into a grade of ethyl alcohol that would meet most of the household's energy needs.

MATERIALS NEEDED

Note: a permit must be obtained from the Bureau of Alcohol, Tobacco, and Firearms before you begin this experiment.

- 6 feet ⅓-inch copper tubing
- coffee can with top and bottom removed
- small bowl
- pressure cooker
- oven thermometer
- 2-gallon plastic container
- 1½ gallons warm sterile water
- 1 cup granulated sugar

- 3 cups pureed apple peelings
- sugar and proof hydrometers
- 1 teaspoon active dried yeast for distilling
- fermentation lock
- cheesecloth
- 4 fuel-burning lamps
- 16 ounces gasoline, benzene, kerosene

EXPERIMENT

A small portion of sugar and apple peelings will be used to simulate a fraction of a household's weekly organic garbage output. These items will then be combined with water and active dried yeast for distilling in a plastic container. This mixture will be allowed to ferment for approximately 4–5 days in a warm, dark environment. The fermented substance will then be placed in a simple pressure-cooker still and be distilled into alcohol. The amount of fuel produced will be measured and multiplied by the weekly output of organic garbage per household to determine the average amount of ethyl alcohol a household could produce. The alcohol will then be tested to compare its burning time and environmental effects to that of more traditional energy fuels.

PROCEDURE

Part A—Build the Still

1. Apply for a permit from the local Bureau of Alcohol, Tobacco, and Firearms to produce a small portion of ethyl alcohol for home experimentation.

2. Begin your experiment by constructing a simple pressure-cooker still. Coil half of the copper tubing five times (leaving the other half attached) and fit it within the coffee can so that the end of the coil bends down and out of the bottom of the can into a bowl. Extend the remaining 3 feet of copper tubing in an arc over to the pressure cooker. The end of the tubing should hook over the top of the stem on the cooker's lid.

3. Remove the pin from the lid of the pressure cooker and place the oven thermometer in its place (this will measure the temperature of the alcohol within the pot). Put the still aside.

Part B—Ferment the Organic Garbage

1. Fill the 2-gallon plastic container ¾ full with warm water. Add 1 cup of sugar and 3 cups of pureed apple peelings. This entire mixture, which is called a mash, should consist of exactly 20% sugar from the cup of table sugar (sucrose) and the sugar found naturally in the apple peelings (fructose). This percentage can be accurately determined by placing the sugar hydrometer into the mash.

2. Mix these items well and add a level teaspoon of active dried yeast for distilling to the mash. Cover the container and place the fermentation lock in the lid of the container. The lock will indicate when fermentation has begun and when it has ended. Place the entire unit in a warm, dark environment at around 80° Fahrenheit (such as a furnace room) to ferment for about 4–5 days. If there are bubbles in the fermentation lock, then fermentation is occurring; if there are no bubbles in the lock, then fermentation has ceased.

Part C—Distill the Fermented Mash

1. After fermentation, strain the mash through a cheesecloth and measure the amount of liquid yield and its alcohol proof with the proof hydrometer. Then place the liquid into the pot of the pressure cooker and attach the lid with its copper coil system that you built in Part A. Place the still unit onto a stove and heat the contents to about 173° Fahrenheit (the temperature at which alcohol boils). Open a window or a vent to provide proper ventilation of the fumes.

2. During this distillation process, the alcohol vapors running through the coils will condense within the coffee can and come out of the other end of the copper coil into the bowl. Measure the proof of this alcohol with the proof hydrometer and pour it back into the pot again to be distilled a second time in order to attain an even higher proof. Repeat this process until you have achieved the highest possible proof of alcohol from your still.

3. Measure the amount of alcohol fuel you have produced with the 2 gallons of mash. Multiply this figure by the amount of mash that could be produced by several families during a week. Then average your figures to calculate the mean amount of alcohol that could be produced by the average household.

4. Next prepare four fuel-burning lamps that will each burn the same amount of alcohol, gasoline, benzene, and kerosene individually. Time the longevity of their flames to see which one lasts the longest. Note which one creates the least amount of smoke and odorous fumes.

RESULTS

1. What was the highest proof you were able to obtain in your alcohol?

2. How much alcohol was produced from 2 gallons of mash? From your calculations, how much alcohol could be produced weekly from the organic garbage of an average household?

3. Which fuel burned the longest and most efficiently? How long would the average weekly household yield of alcohol last? Would this satisfy most of the household's energy needs? How does alcohol as a fuel source compare to the traditional fuels?

Can CMOS Logic, Rather Than a Potentiometer, Regulate Voltage?

PURPOSE

To design and construct a variable power supply with three programmable presets that can regulate up to 30 volts of direct current. This voltage would be controlled by CMOS logic, which would vary the amount of resistance needed to ground to the regulator's adjust pin.

MATERIALS NEEDED

Note: Engineering and troubleshooting experience is required for this project.

- instructions for designing and building an unregulated power supply
- wooden box (1 square foot)
- socket board
- oscilloscope with memory
- vom (volt-ohmmeter)
- copper circuit boards
- proto board and hook up wire to build the circuitry
- Phillips-head screw driver
- standard screw driver
- nut driver set

- drill with assorted bits
- multimeter with leads
- hacksaw with blades
- assorted screws with matching nuts
- assorted electronic components (switches and resistors)

EXPERIMENT

A variable power supply will be designed and built with three preset voltages. The voltages will be varied by a logic-controlled push button network. This network will also be used to control the amount of resistance, instead of a potentiometer, which is usually inefficient because it is rough and sometimes skips. With fixed resistors of a given value, the resistance that is being placed on a circuit and the exact voltage output could be accurately computed. Another reason for selecting the logic control over the potentiometer is because it provides a push button control for a number of fixed voltage references, which cannot be done with a potentiometer.

PROCEDURE

1. Design an unregulated power supply from instructions in an engineering book.

2. Following the instructions, design the switching circuitry. Then plan the layout of the box that will house the unregulated power supply and the switching circuitry.
   cuitry.

3. Then, build the circuits on an experimenter's socket board so that later repairs and modifications will be made easier.

4. After the circuits are set up, troubleshoot them by putting an oscilloscope and a volt/ohmmeter in key parts of the circuits to observe their reactions with the circuit.

5. Next, design the etching plans for the copper circuit boards. This will require the planning of the component layout for the easiest etching pattern of the circuit.

6. Etch the copper circuit boards for the rectifier and filter circuit in the unregulated supply and proceed to drill, mount and solder the components onto the boards.

7. Mount the assemblies into the box and connect the required wiring. Then, test the circuits several times to make sure that they work properly. All necessary repairs and modifications should be made.

8. Finally, mount meter and push buttons on the front panel of the box that will house the unregulated power supply and begin testing.

RESULTS

1. Did you find any problems in your original design? What design changes did you make to correct the problems?

2. Did your final circuit operate according to your initial calculations on both an open circuit and under load conditions?

3. After how much wattage did the regulator flatten out? Is this the standard maximum?

The Robotic-Assisted Plotter

PURPOSE

To build a robot capable of drawing different shapes onto paper by using information supplied by a computer.

MATERIALS NEEDED

Note: This project will require some computer programming and engineering experience.

- 1 robot shell—made from the Robotix brand toy
- 4 robot motors—made from the Robotix brand toy
- 4 motor sensors—"optical shaft encoders" (an infrared emmitter/detector set with slotted disk)
- experimental computer system—Apple II+ //e. or //gs by Apple Computer, Inc.
- formatted disk (Dos 3.3 or Prodos)
- computer language—Applesoft Basic by Apple Computer, Inc. in Dos 3.3 (can be easily converted to Prodos)

- computer interface:
  ribbon cable from game port of computer to control circuit
- control circuit components:
  2 three-line to eight-line decoder chips (74LS139)
  2 hex inverter chips (74LS04)
  2 quad (4) input and gate chips (74LS20)
  2 dual (2) input and gate chips (74LS08)
  2 triple (3) input and gate chips (74LS11)
  6 optoisolator (high gain) (4370)

4 SPST-Relays (5 volts) (motor on-off)

2 DPDT-Relays (5 volts) (motor direction)

4 resistors (1k) (optos)

4 resistors (330 ohms) (LEDs)

4 LEDs (monitor control states-lights)

4 dip switches (for running manual tests with circuit only)

EXPERIMENT

A method of building a robot will be created. The robot should be able to draw pictures of shapes that are created on a computer screen. In addition, a program that will command the robot to draw will be developed.

PROCEDURE

1. Create a computer drawing program that can draw lines and squares. The program should allow you to be able to load and save the shapes onto a disk. Thus, using the Applesoft Basic, you will have to write a program to command the computer to turn on a graphics display screen and set up the screen and menu. This menu should include options for drawing the required shapes and saving and loading the information describing the shapes.

2. After a user chooses an option, the computer will go to one of the modules of the program as listed by the menu. The first module would draw the shapes, in two selectable colors, onto the screen using the user's input. The statistics of the shape will then be saved, and then others may be drawn. The other modules (the saving and loading modules) will require the program to save the statistics in an array variable into a text file on the disk, read them back when loaded, and redisplay the shapes.

3. Next, another program will be written to make the robot draw the shapes onto the paper. This will require the program to first set up the robot. The robot will be commanded (through the control circuit) to move from one edge of the paper to the other edge. Then by measuring the distance the robot traveled in each direction by the number of slots seen by the optical shaft encoders, it could find out the scale of the paper by comparing it to the scale on the screen. This will tell the robot the size of the shapes to be drawn.

4. Next, the program must load the picture, which was saved on disk under a certain file name. Then, the program must take the first shape's data (start points, end points, and color) and examine it. The program must first determine where the shape is, and move the robot there. Then, it must determine the angle of the shape and turn

the robot to that angle. Thus, if the program determines the angle to be 180 degrees it would instruct the robot to put down the appropriate pen and move straight to the end of the shape (that is, a line). The robot must then pick up the pen and calculate the next shape. It would continue this way until all shapes are done.

5. Since the computer only has four on and off 5-volt outputs and four directional outputs, you must design an interface circuit to carry out the various commands given to the motors. Therefore, in a circuit which multiplexes, using logic circuits, four computer outputs must be made into 16 states. These states will then be connected in such a way as to turn on and off direction-controlling and on-off state-controlling relays. (An optoisolator must be used to protect the circuit from relay feedback and high current.) The relays will control the motors so as to allow the robot to move and pick up and put down the attached pens.

6. Attach the optical shaft encoders and disks to the robot. The optical shaft encoders must be able to shine light through the disks and receive light on the other side of the encoder. The disk must be attached so that it spins at the same rate, time, and direction as the motor moves. The slot must be made so that the disk moves from one slot to the next while the motor moves a certain amount. The information from the optical shaft encoder will let the computer know the position of the robot and the pens. This will be used by the robot to know the robot's status.

7. Test the logic circuits in the interface to make sure they operate as directed. If there are any errors in the design and construction they must be corrected.

8. The programs must be tested to see if they work correctly.

9. Test the new circuit for any quirks.

10. Test the sensors for compatibility.

11. Put the program and robot into action to see if they can work together to draw geometric shapes.

(Definitions of some of these words can be found in an electronics encyclopedia.)

RESULTS

1. Was there a quirk in the new circuit? If so, was it due to an incompatibility in the sensors?

2. Could the robot have been programmed to draw geometric shapes other than lines and squares?

3. From your developments with the robotic-assisted plotter, what other applications do you suppose it can be used for?

18 The Effects of Industrial Pollutants in the Environment of the Convict Cichlid Fish

PURPOSE

To determine how chemical industrial wastes that already come into contact with local urban fish, would temporarily affect a tropical fish, the Convict Cichlid. In addition, to find out how much of each pollutant can be added per liter of water to calculate the concentrations that can be tolerated by the fish before any adverse effects are noticed.

MATERIALS NEEDED

- 7 5-liter fish tanks (3 will serve as experimental tanks, 3 as nonexperimental holding tanks, and 1 as the control)
- 35 liters distilled water
- 7 fish tank heaters
- 7 filters
- 2 thermometers
- 8 Convict Cichlid fish
- dropper
- industrial pollutants (20 cc each of sulfuric acid, chlorine bleach, and copper sulfate)

EXPERIMENT

Two Convict Cichlid fish will be placed in each of four 5-liter fish tanks. Three experimental tanks will be exposed to different amounts of pollutants, while the fourth tank will serve as the control and not be exposed to pollutants. The behavior, color, movement, and rate of respiration of each fish will be observed.

PROCEDURE

1. Set up the 5-liter fish tanks. Be sure that the same distilled water is used in each and that its temperature is around 78° Fahrenheit.
2. Put two Convict Cichlids into each of the three experimental tanks and two fish into a fourth, control tank. Allow them to adapt to the environment for about 5 minutes.
3. Use the dropper to gradually add 1 cc of one pollutant to the first experimental tank.
4. Observe and compare both the first experimental tank and the control tank of fish. Note changes in the experimental groups' behavior, color, movement, and rate of respiration (calculate by counting the number of times the gills move per minute). If there are no noticeable changes with 1 cc of the pollutant, add another and continue adding until you begin to see an adverse reaction from the first experimental group of fish.
5. Remove the fish from the first experimental tank and put them into their own labeled 5-liter holding tank of distilled water. Repeat Steps 3–5 with a different pollutant for both the second and third tanks.

RESULTS

1. What was the maximum amount of each pollutant that could be administered without any adverse effects on the fish? At what level of pollutant concentration did the fish noticeably react?
2. Compare the color of the experimental groups to that of the control group. Were there any differences? What pollutant affected this characteristic the most (if at all)?
3. Compare the overall behavior of the fish. Did the pollutants induce or reduce their movements at higher levels?
4. After the experimental Convict Cichlids were returned to a pure environment, did they return to normal, or did they undergo further changes in their behavior?
5. What do your results tell you about the adapatability and resistance of these tropical fish to industrial pollutants? Do you believe that they are as tolerant as local urban fish?

20

Can Limestone Be Used to Protect Pine Trees from Acid Rain?

PURPOSE

To determine if limestone, which is used to enrich soil so that grass and shrubbery may grow healthier, could protect pine trees from acid rain.

MATERIALS NEEDED

- ◆ 4 potted pine trees (about 2 feet in height and of the same age)
- ◆ 16 ounces limestone (can be obtained from a nursery)
- ◆ 96 ounces of a simulated acid rain solution (90% water/10% sulfuric acid) (enough to water each tree twice a week for four weeks)

EXPERIMENT

The soil of two potted pine trees will be fertilized with varying portions of limestone and then sprinkled with the simulated acid rain solution. Two other trees will serve as the controls, with one receiving the acid rain solution only and the other receiving the limestone only. The acid rain solution will be given to each tree periodically for 4 weeks together with the limestone. The two controls will receive either the acid rain solution or the limestone only.

PROCEDURE

1. Label each tree as *Experimental 1, Experimental 2, Control 1,* and *Control 2*.

2. Apply ½ oz of the limestone to the soil of *Experimental 1,* 1 oz to the soil of *Experimental 2,* and ¾ oz to *Control 1* (no limestone will

be given to *Control 2*). Each tree (with the exception of *Control 1*) will then be sprinkled with 4 oz of the simulated acid rain solution.

3. One day each week, repeat the same doses of limestone you gave to the trees. Two days each week, give 6 oz of the acid rain solution to the trees (with the exception of *Control 1.*) Give the experimental trees their portion on the same day they will receive the limestone treatments.

4. Record the reactions of the trees on a daily basis for four weeks.

RESULTS

1. What were the overall conditions of the plants after experimentation? Was the experimental pair that was treated with limestone in better condition than the control that was not?

2. Did the control that received only limestone appear healthy or damaged?

3. What combination of limestone (½ oz or 1 oz) per 6 oz acid rain solution yielded the most favorable results?

21

What Section of a Town Has the Most Pollution in the Form of Airborne Particles?

PURPOSE

To determine which section of any given town contains the most airborne particles as pollution.

MATERIALS NEEDED

- 30 3" × 5" index cards
- petroleum jelly
- stapler
- 30 sticks of balsa wood or wooden dowels
- magnifying glass
- plastic wrap

EXPERIMENT

Index cards smeared with petroleum jelly will be used to collect samples of airborne particles from 10 designated locations of a town. Three samples will be taken at each location under different types of weather conditions—clear and calm, windy, and hot and humid.

PROCEDURE

1. Select 10 test locations in a particular town and write the name of each location on a separate index card.
2. Draw a circle on 10 of the 3 × 5 index cards and smear them with petroleum jelly. Next, staple each card to a balsa wood stick or wooden dowel and place each stick in the ground at each of 10 predetermined town locations for 48 hours under clear and calm weather conditions.

3. After the 48 hours, collect all the sticks and count every particle within the circles using a magnifying glass. Record your results for each location, wrap the cards individually in clear plastic wrap and store them carefully.

4. Repeat Steps 1 and 3 again under windy weather conditions and under hot and humid conditions. (If rainfall should occur, the samples must be retaken.) Record all your results.

5. After all the particle collections are made, average the three results for each location to arrive at a standard number for each particular site.

RESULTS

1. Which site collected the most airborne particles under all three weather conditions?

2. Which type of the three weather conditions seemed to bring about the most airborne particles? The least?

3. Try to identify the airborne particles and their sources.

4. Did the airborne particles that were found in one location appear to be the same as those found in another location? If so, which type of particle seemed to be the most airborne?

22

Environmental Effects on the Biodegradability of Plastic Bags, Paper Bags, and Newspaper

Note: This experiment requires a time period of at least 3 months.

PURPOSE

To test several types of plastic bags in different environments to determine if or how fast they decompose in comparison to paper bags and newspaper in the same environments.

MATERIALS NEEDED

- 8 biodegradable plastic bags (use two different brands)
- 8 nonbiodegradable plastic bags (use two different brands)
- 4 brown paper bags
- 4 pages of newspaper
- 3 nets (plastic or cotton)
- wire or string
- 6 wooden posts
- mulch pile—approximately 4 feet high (consisting of grass clippings and leaves with rotting vegetable matter, fertilizer, and compost starter culture) in a 6-foot diameter ring made of wire fencing material
- leaf pile—approximately 3 feet high
- 8 plastic containers (approximately ½ gallon each)
- tap water
- saltwater (15% by volume)

EXPERIMENT

The biodegradability of several plastic bags, brown paper bags and newspaper will be tested in different environmental conditions: direct sunlight, a mulch pile (which simulates an active landfill), a leaf pile (which simulates a dry landfill), tap water (which simulates a lake), and in saltwater (which simulates an ocean).

PROCEDURE

1. Fold and secure two types of biodegradable and nonbiodegradable plastic bags on top of a net with wire or string. Tie a wooden post at each end of the net and place each post into the ground, leaving the plastic bags exposed to the sun. Do the same with one paper bag and a page of newspaper.

2. Place two types of biodegradable and nonbiodegradable plastic bags, a piece of newspaper, and a brown paper bag in the middle of the mulch pile. Wet the pile thoroughly with water.

3. Place the same types of materials that were used in Step 2 in the middle of the leaf pile.

4. Place two biodegradable plastic bags, two nonbiodegradable plastic bags, one paper bag, and one page of newspaper into four separate containers of tap water. Then, place the same types of materials into separate containers of 15% (by volume) saltwater.

5. Allow all the materials to stay in their environments for three months or longer. Record the changes that occurred to the plastic bags, paper bags, and newspapers in the different environments upon removal.

RESULTS

1. Did any of the materials decompose? If so, which materials decomposed most thoroughly?

2. Was the rate of degradation greatest in the exposure to the sunlight, mulch pile, leaf pile, tap water, or saltwater?

3. Did the plastic bags that were advertised as biodegradable appear any different from the nonbiodegradable bags?

23

How Does Acid Rain Affect the Cell Structure of *Spirogyra?*

PURPOSE

To determine whether water that contains a measurable level of acid—with a pH level below 7 (to simulate acid rain)—will affect the cellular structure of *Spirogyra,* a common freshwater algae of the phylum Chlorophyta.

MATERIALS NEEDED

- 3 *Spirogyra* algae cultures
- 3 1-gallon fishbowls
- 6 liters distilled water
- 1 liter soil/water mixture (5 milligrams soil and 1 liter nondistilled water)
- 3 lamps, each with 40-watt bulb
- thermometer
- concave microscope slides
- 200× microscope
- pH indicator
- dropper
- 15 cubic centimeters of 90% water and 10% sulfuric acid

EXPERIMENT

Cultures of *Spirogyra* will be grown in three separate fishbowls. One will contain healthy algae cultivated in pollution-free water. Another fishbowl will contain healthy algae cultivated in a low-acid water solution (water in which a low concentrate of acid was added to bring the pH to a level of 6.0). The third fishbowl will contain healthy algae cultivated in a high-acid water solution (water in which a high concentrate of acid was added to bring the pH to a level of 3.0). Specimens from each tank will be drawn daily and observed with a 200× microscope. These observations will be recorded and labeled.

PROCEDURE

1. Place *Spirogyra* cultures in three 1-gallon fishbowls. The bowls should contain 2 liters of distilled water and equal amounts of the healthy *Spirogyra* cultures. Then, add an equal amount of the soil/water mixture to each bowl to promote rapid algae growth. Place each bowl under a 40-watt lamp and heat to 20° Celsius.

2. Observe and record the algae growth daily.

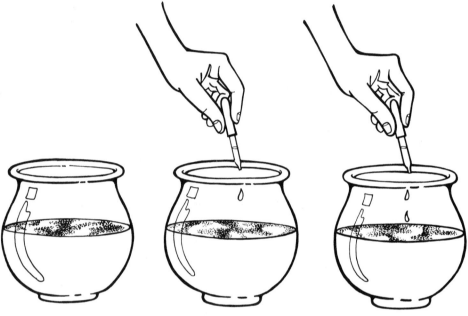

Bowl 1 will be left with the neutral solution of water and healthy algae.

Bowl 2 will contain 3 cc of the water and 10% sulfuric acid solution to equal a low acid solution with a pH of 6.0.

Bowl 3 will contain 12 cc of the water and 10% sulfuric acid solution to equal a high acid solution with a pH of 3.0.

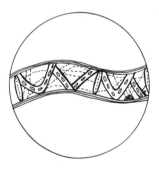

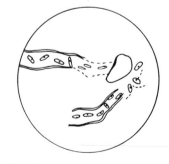

On day 3, the cell structure of the algae from Bowl 1 should be normal.

On day 3, the cell structure of the algae from Bowl 2 should show some signs of deterioration.

On day 3, the cell structure of the algae from Bowl 3 should be under complete destruction.

3. When the algae appear healthy and abundant, take a sample from each tank and observe it on slides under the microscope. Be sure to label the samples from the specific bowl from which they were taken.

4. Allow the algae to grow under optimum laboratory conditions for 10 days. On the tenth day, take another sample from each of the three bowls and observe them on slides under the microscope. Measure the pH level of the water, using the pH Indicator. A neutral solution should be found in each bowl.

5. *Acid Rain Day 1:* The acid will now be administered to the bowls. (Bowl 1 will be left with the neutral solution of water and healthy algae.) With the dropper, add 3 cc of a mixture of water and 10% sulfuric acid (low acid solution to measure a pH of 6.0) into Bowl 2. Into Bowl 3, add 12 cc of a mixture of water and 10% sulfuric acid (high acid solution to measure a pH of 3.0). Immediately take an algae sample from these two bowls for microscopic viewing, and draw and label the results.

6. *Acid Rain Day 2:* 24 hours after the simulated acid rain has entered the water supply of the *Spirogyra,* take samples of the algae again from each bowl (including the control) and observe them under the microscope. Note any changes in the algae cell structure. Draw and label what you see.

7. *Acid Rain Day 3:* 48 hours after the simulated acid rain has entered the water supply of the *Spirogyra,* take algae samples from each bowl (including the control) and observe them under the microscope. Note any increased cellular changes. Again, draw and label what you see.

8. Compare the differences in the cell structures between the three samples for the 3-day period.

RESULTS

1. Locate a diagram of a typical, healthy *Spirogyra* cell. Is this diagram consistent with your final drawing of Bowl 1? Compare this diagram with your final drawings from Bowls 2 and 3. Were there any changes at all in the structure of the algae? If so, what part of the algaes' cellular structure has been altered?

2. What conclusions can be drawn from the effects that the simulated acid rain had on the *Spirogyra?* Was this simulation comparable to actual acid rain? What other acids mights be used to simulate the rain?

3. If *Spirogyra* is in fact vulnerable to acid rain (as your experimental results may indicate), will there eventually be changes in the food chain that might affect higher forms of life?

24

Common Cold Remedies: Are They Helpful?

PURPOSE

There are cold viruses that are comprised of both a viral infection coexisting with a bacterial infection. This project will try to isolate the bacterial portion of nasal washings from an individual afflicted with a cold virus comprised of both a viral and bacterial infection, to determine whether popular cold remedies have any effect in eliminating the bacterial portion.

MATERIALS NEEDED

- nasal cultures of a person infected with a viral/bacterial cold
- 6 petri dishes: tryptic soy agar (TSA) with 5% sheep blood
- moist sterile applicators
- 8-ounce plastic cups
- warm sterile water
- zinc (tablet)
- aspirin (any brand, regular strength)
- nonaspirin pain reliever
- liquid vitamin C
- chicken soup
- sterile filter paper disks
- incubator with thermometer
- Gram's stain test materials: (glass slides, Bunsen burner, crystal violet solution, tap water, safranine, microscope with oil-immersion lens)

EXPERIMENT

The nasal washings of a person afflicted with a viral/bacterial cold will be streaked onto six individually marked petri dishes. Five dishes will then be covered with sterile filter-paper disks individually soaked in a different cold remedy solution. The dishes will be covered, inverted, and placed in an incubator for 48 hours (this will be the experimental group). The remaining dish will not be covered with a filter disk (this will be the control).

PROCEDURE

1. For each of six TSA petri dishes place a moist sterile applicator into the nose of an infected person for a few seconds to absorb nasal secretions. Streak the applicator onto a petri dish and repeat for the five remaining petri dishes. Then label the six dishes according to the cold remedy they will be treated with.

2. Pour each cold remedy into an 8-ounce cup. Dissolve any nonliquid remedies completely in warm sterile water. Dip sterile filter paper disks into each solution and place them individually on each of the streaked petri dishes. One petri dish will not receive a solution, (the control).

3. Cover and invert all of the petri dishes and put them in an incubator at 37° Celsius for 48 hours.

4. After 48 hours, remove the petri dishes from the incubator and compare the effects of each cold remedy solution to the control.

5. Do a Gram's stain for each dish to determine whether the bacteria from each was gram-positive or gram-negative cocci or bacilli (see Steps 8–11 in Project 37).

RESULTS

1. What type of bacteria was present, gram-positive or gram-negative?

2. Did any of the remedies have any effect upon the bacteria? If so, which one was the most effective?

3. Could the bacteria from other individuals with the dual infection possibly react differently toward the cold remedies?

What Substance Is Most Effective for Cleaning Teeth?

PURPOSE

To determine which tooth cleaner is the most effective in protecting teeth from sugars and acids that dimineralize and decalcify tooth enamel.

MATERIALS NEEDED

- 12 extracted molars (approximately the same age and in good condition, available from a dentist's office)
- water
- 12 empty petri dishes
- soda pop
- lemon juice
- toothbrush
- baking soda
- mouthwash
- fluoridated toothpaste
- nonfluoridated toothpaste
- tartar-control toothpaste

EXPERIMENT

Twelve different molars will be exposed to acids and sugars for a period of two weeks. Each of 10 teeth will be cleaned daily with one of the cleaners. The two remaining teeth will serve as the control. They will be placed in the soda pop and lemon juice respectively and will be brushed with water only. At the end of three weeks the condition of the molars will be carefully observed to determine which substance worked the best as a cleaner and provided the greatest protection.

PROCEDURE

1. Obtain 12 molars that are approximately the same age from a dentist's office.

2. Rinse the teeth with boiling water and dry them thoroughly.

3. Fill six empty petri dishes ¾ full with soda pop. Then fill another six empty petri dishes ¾ full with lemon juice.

4. Place a molar into each dish, cover it, and label it according to the type of solution with which it will be brushed. For example, begin by labeling one molar in the soda pop solution *SP—baking soda* and one molar in the lemon juice solution *LJ—baking soda,* and so on.

5. Soak each tooth in its solution for 24 hours. Then remove the teeth individually and brush them with the substance that is labeled on their particular dishes. After cleaning, return the teeth to their petri dishes, cover, and repeat the same procedure daily for three weeks. At the end of the period observe the condition of each tooth. Look for signs of deterioration and discoloring.

RESULTS

1. Did any of the teeth show signs of deterioration and discoloring? If so, what changes did you observe. Were these changes consistent among all the teeth, or did they vary?

2. Which substance, soda pop or lemon juice, had the greatest impact, if any, on the molars?

3. Which substance, if any, kept the teeth clean and protected the longest? Does this result agree or disagree with what your dentist recommends as a tooth cleaner?

26

Are There Really Any Differences Among Commercial Hand Lotions?

PURPOSE

To determine if there are any differences among commercial hand and body lotions. The experiment will compare their pH levels, densities, and antibacterial effects.

MATERIALS NEEDED

- 10 commercial brands hand and body lotion
- pH indicator test
- 8 plastic 4-ounce measuring cups
- balance scale
- sterile cotton swabs

- human subjects
- petri dishes: tryptic soy agar (TSA) with 5% sheep blood
- sterile plastic gloves
- incubator

EXPERIMENT

Ten commercial hand and body lotions will first be subjected to a pH indicator test to determine if they contain the same levels of acids and bases. Then, the densities of each lotion will be computed and compared to each other. Finally, the lotions will be tested to see if they have any antibacterial qualities.

PROCEDURE

1. Obtain 10 commercial hand and body lotion samples. Perform a pH indicator test on each sample and record their respective pH levels.

2. Weigh one plastic cup and record.

3. Measure the density of each lotion by filling the plastic cup half full with a particular hand and body lotion and weighing it on a balance scale. Then subtract the cup's weight to obtain the mass of the lotion. Find the density of the sample by dividing its mass by its volume (4 oz). Repeat this procedure for the remaining lotions and record your results.

4. Wipe sterile cotton swabs across the forearms of several volunteers and streak them onto labeled petri dishes. Then put on a pair of sterile plastic gloves and rub a $\frac{1}{2}$-teaspoon of a different lotion onto each volunteer's forearm. Be sure to change gloves between applications. After the lotions have been absorbed into their forearms for about five minutes, wipe another sterile applicator across the forearms again and streak them onto labeled petri dishes. Cover all the petri dishes and incubate them for 48 hours.

RESULTS

1. Compare the pH levels and densities of all the lotions. Were they comparable or did they differ? If they differed, how much of a variation existed?

2. Compare the bacteria present in the petri dishes from the volunteers before and after the application of the lotions. Did any of the lotions have an effect in reducing or eliminating the amount of bacteria present?

The Relationship Between Alcohol Dosage and Dependency in a Rat

Note: This experiment must be conducted under the supervision of a research scientist.

PURPOSE

To determine the effects of various, physically tolerable levels of alcohol exposure in rats by analyzing their behavioral responses and related blood alcohol levels.

MATERIALS NEEDED

- 12 laboratory rats
- 4 airtight inhalation chambers
- ethanol/oxygen vaporization, metering and pumping equipment
- rat food and water
- enzyme assay equipment (for determining the blood-alcohol levels in the rats)
- trichloroacetic acid
- Ependorf tubes
- microcentrifuge
- alcohol dehydrogenase and nicotinamide adenine dinucleotide
- glycine buffer
- spectrophotometer

EXPERIMENT

Twelve rats will be divided into three groups of four and placed individually in airtight inhalation chambers. Three rats from each group will be exposed to a controlled rate of alcohol vaporization (the experimental group), while the remaining rat will not (the control rat). Over a period of time, blood samples will be obtained from the tail veins of each rat and an enzyme assay test will be conducted to determine the average blood-alcohol levels in each rat. After the rats have been exposed for 3 days, they will be removed from their environments. About 6 hours later, the withdrawal symptoms of the rats will be observed for tail tremors, tail stiffening, body tremors, and body rigidity. The experiment will be repeated on Groups 2 and 3 at higher levels of alcohol vaporization.

PROCEDURE

1. Obtain permission to work under the supervision of a research scientist, probably at a local university.

2. Set up inhalation chambers and connect the ethanol/oxygen vaporizing equipment to three chambers, while connecting the fourth chamber to equipment that will vaporize only oxygen. Be sure to supply food and water for each chamber.

3. Place one rat into each of the four chambers and administer the ethanol/oxygen vaporization and the oxygen vaporization.

4. Keep the rats in their chambers for 3 days. During this period obtain 100 μl of blood from the tail veins of each rat each day with the help of the research scientist and derive the average blood alcohol level of each rat through the enzyme assay procedure.

David Karanian found that even lower levels of blood-alcohol were sufficient to generate alcohol dependency in the rats as measured by their withdrawal symptoms over a 3-day period.

5. To complete the enzyme assay procedure, first deproteinize each blood sample by adding 400 μl of trichloroacetic acid (TCA) to each blood sample in an Ependorf tube. Spin the Ependorf tube for four minutes in a microcentrifuge. This will separate the sample into protein and plasma.

6. Place 100 μl of the plasma into a prepared assay vial containing alcohol dehydrogenase (ADH) and nicotinamide adenine dinucleotide (NAD). Add 3 ml of glycine buffer to the vial. Insert the vial and allow it to sit for 30 minutes.

7. Place the vial in a spectrophotometer and set the visible light wavelength to 340 nm. The higher the alcohol content in the vial, the lower the light emission when placed in the spectrophotometer. These measurements will result in a reading that translates to the appropriate percentages of blood alcohol level.

8. After the third day, remove and separate the first group of experimental rats and the control rat. Compare all symptoms of nervousness and withdrawal immediately and after a 6-hour period.

9. Repeat the same procedures for the second and third groups of rats. However, Group 2 should be exposed to a slightly higher amount of ethanol vapors than Group 1, and Group 3 should be exposed to slightly higher amounts of ethanol vapors than Group 2.

RESULTS

1. What physical changes were visible in each rat after exposure? After 6 hours? Were there any noticeable differences between the experimental and the control groups?

2. What were the average blood-alcohol levels in each rat? In a particular group? In the entire experimental group?

3. Were there variations among the blood-alcohol levels of the rats?

4. What percentage of blood-alcohol was needed over a 3-day period in order to generate dependency in the rats as measured by withdrawal symptoms?

5. Do you believe from this experiment that it was the amount of ethanol vaporization administered or the continuous exposure to the alchol over the 3 days that was related to dependency?

6. Can you apply your findings to binge drinking in the human population?

How Effective Are Various Items in Protecting Against Ultraviolet Radiation?

PURPOSE

To use an organism such as a bacterium to simulate a human body in order to determine the effectiveness of items commonly used to protect against ultraviolet radiation.

MATERIALS NEEDED

♦ sterile cotton swabs

♦ nutrient broth culture of a bacteria (*Serratia marcescens*)

♦ 5 tryptic soy agar (TSA) plates with 5% sheep blood (more plates will be needed if more than three items will be tested)

♦ ultraviolet lamp

♦ various items used to protect the body against ultraviolet radiation, such as clothing, sunglasses, and sunscreen lotion

EXPERIMENT

TSA plates with 5% sheep blood will be smeared with the bacteria *Serratia marcescens* and allowed to cultivate. Various items to be tested, such as clothing, sunglasses, and sunscreen lotion, will be placed over the bacteria as a protective covering from the ultraviolet radiation that the plates will be exposed to.

PROCEDURE

1. With a sterile cotton swab, place the culture of bacteria on the entire surface of each of the five agar plates and allow it to cultivate.

After the nutrient agar plants are covered with the bacteria, items normally used in the sun (such as sunglasses) will be placed on the plate to determine if they can actually protect the bacteria from the ultraviolet rays.

2. Cover the entire surface (if possible) of three plates with the items being tested—for example, clothing, glasses, and sunscreen. To do the sunscreen test, first smear the lotion on clear plastic wrap and then wrap the plastic over the plate. Leave two plates uncovered to serve as the control (one plate will be unexposed to the ultraviolet lamp, while the other will be exposed to the ultraviolet lamp).

3. Place the three covered plates plus one of the uncovered plates directly underneath the ultraviolet lamp for 2 minutes of exposure. Then turn off the light and remove the coverings from each dish. Cover these four exposed plates and the unexposed plate with a lid and put the plates away in a dark area at room temperature overnight.

4. Observe the condition of the bacteria after 24 hours and record your observations.

RESULTS

1. Compare the population and color of bacteria on the experimental plates exposed to ultraviolet light to that of the control groups. Is there any difference between the protected and exposed plates, or between the unprotected/exposed and unprotected/unexposed plates?

2. Which item offered the most protection against ultraviolet radiation? Which offered the least?

3. Compare colored and colorless testing items. Did the colored items have any effect on ultraviolet penetration? Compare the thickness of the materials. Did thicker testing materials offer better protection against the ultraviolet radiation than the thinner materials?

4. Did the sunscreen lotion offer good protection? Based on the data from this experiment, do you think that most people are well protected against ultraviolet radiation?

29

The Effect of Caffeine on the Development and Survival of Mealworms

PURPOSE

To determine the effects of varying doses of caffeine on mealworms by noting their behavior, food intake, and rate of reproduction.

MATERIALS NEEDED

- 6 cups chopped food (oat-meal, fruits and vegetables)*
- knife
- 50–75 milligrams caffeine (use 4 ounces water mixed with 2 teaspoons regular instant cof-fee as a substitute)*
- 400–500 milligrams caffeine [use 3 or 4 stimulant pills (such as No Doz or Vivarin brand) dissolved in 4 ounces of water as a substitute]*
- distilled water
- 45 mealworm larvae
- scale (measures in grams)
- 3 square plastic containers (8" × 8" × 6")
- 3 metal screens to serve as aer-ated covers

*Note: You will need to prepare another mixture of these ingredients after the mealworms develop.

EXPERIMENT

The mealworms will be divided into three equal groups. Group A will be exposed to low levels of caffeine by eating food moistened with the 4 oz of instant coffee. Group B will be exposed to high levels of caffeine by eating food moistened with the 4 oz of stimulant pill mixture. Group C will serve as a control group and will eat food moistened by 4 oz of pure water only.

PROCEDURE

1. Prepare food by chopping and mixing into small bits. For Group A, moisten 2 cups of chopped food with 4 oz of instant regular coffee and blend into a uniform consistency. For Group B, prepare caffeine mixture by dissolving 3 or 4 stimulant pills in 4 oz of warm water. Then, blend with 2 cups of food. For Group C, blend 4 oz of water with 2 cups of food.

2. Divide the worms into three equal groups. Then, weigh each larvae in Group A in grams and average their weights to come up with the approximate average weight of Group A. Do the same for Groups B and C and record all figures.

3. Put Group A into the container with a low level of caffeine. Put Group B into the container with a high level of caffeine. Put Group C into the container with no caffeine. Then, weigh each unit as a whole and record. Next, cover each container with a metal screen.

4. Chart the activity of the worms until they pupate. Record food intake, behavior changes, rates of pupating, and the death rate.

5. After most of the worms form into adults, weigh each unit as a whole again and record. Then, remove the adults of each group (keeping them separate), and obtain a group weight average. Then,

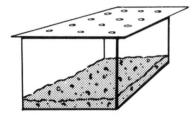

Group A will be exposed to low levels of caffeine by eating food moistened with 4 oz of instant coffee.

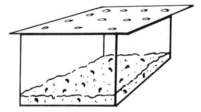

Group B will be exposed to high levels of caffeine by eating food moistened with 4 oz of stimulant pill mixture.

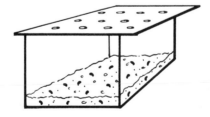

Group C will serve as a control and will eat food moistened with 4 oz of distilled water only.

dispose of all old contents and refill the three containers again in the same manner as before. Then, return Groups A, B, and C back to their clean containers with the same caffeine exposure. Again, weigh each unit as a whole and record.

6. Now chart the adults' activity for approximately 5 days. Record the same information as you did when they were in the larva stage. At the end of the 5 days, weigh each unit as a whole again, and each individual adult.

RESULTS

1. Compare the weights of the larvae to the young adults and older adults. Did they change much among their group? Did they change between groups? Which group weighed the most? The least?

2. Which group ate the most? The least? Do you believe that caffeine influenced their food intake?

3. Comparing their overall behavior, did the caffeine induce their activity at higher levels? Were smaller doses in fact more toxic? Do smaller doses slow down molting into reproductive adults?

4. Can you make any further conclusions?

30

The Wave, the Golden Mean, and $r = \left[\dfrac{2}{(-1 + \sqrt{5})} \right]^\wedge \theta$

Note: Knowledge and experience in analytical geometry and computer programming are required for this project.

PURPOSE

To determine if there is any possible relationship between the origami fold known as "The Wave" and the Golden Mean or ratio, the numerical value of which is $(\frac{1 + \sqrt{5}}{2})$. This will be accomplished by determining the equation of the wave's spirals.

MATERIALS NEEDED

♦ 4 sheets 30-centimeter square origami paper (or more)
♦ 1 sheet 50 centimeter square origami paper
♦ 2 sheets graph paper
♦ Macintosh Plus computer with 2 megabytes of memory
♦ Microsoft QuickBASIC© software

EXPERIMENT

The origami paper will be folded into the patterns known as "waves." Each pattern will use a different number of divisions to demonstrate the effects of this on the resulting model. A geometric analysis will be performed to derive equations that describe characteristics of the folded models. Measurements of the models will be taken to be used as data to be related by polar equations. A basic program will be written on a Macin-

An International Science and Engineering Fair Project

tosh Plus computer with the use of Microsoft QuickBASIC software, to draw polar spirals of the logarithmic or equiangular variety, which will be adjusted to match the spirals found in the wave.

PROCEDURE

1. Fold each of the sheets of paper following the instructions in the diagram, each time using 3, 6, and 12 divisions. Observe the effect this has on the resolution and shape of the model. Try folding another with an uneven number of divisions (for example, 16ths at the point, moving to 8ths at the outer edges). Record your observations.

2. Carefully examine the structure of the resulting folds. Derive equations for the angles between consecutive secants of each spiral, as a function of the number of the division from the tip of "The Wave," taking the tip to be fold #0. Try to use these equations to determine a polar equation describing the spirals.

3. Practice folding the wave a few more times. Then, fold a model using 32 divisions with the 50-cm paper. If necessary, use a ruler to make straight creases.

4. Create a polar axis in the center of one of the sheets of graph paper. Draw a radius every .25 π radians of rotation. Taking the point of

International Science and Engineering Fair finalist Matthew Green and his project.

117

The Wave

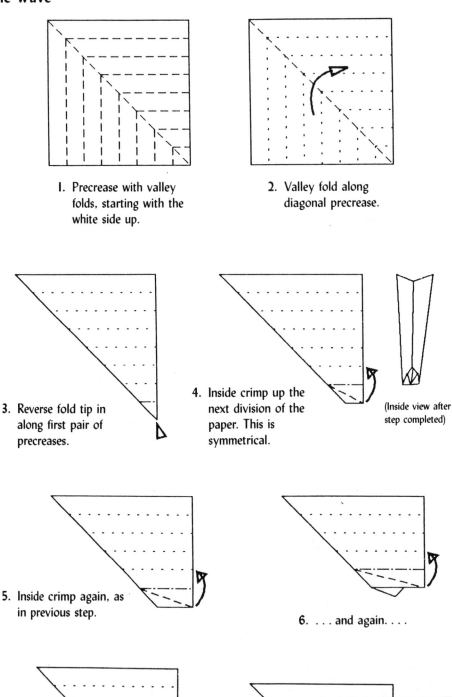

1. Precrease with valley folds, starting with the white side up.

2. Valley fold along diagonal precrease.

3. Reverse fold tip in along first pair of precreases.

4. Inside crimp up the next division of the paper. This is symmetrical.

(Inside view after step completed)

5. Inside crimp again, as in previous step.

6. . . . and again. . . .

7. . . . and again. . . .

8.

118

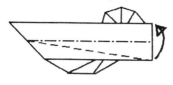

9.

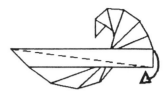

10. Valley fold down the
flaps.

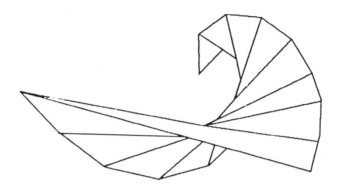

"The Wave" as the origin, trace the outline of the outer spiral of the wave onto the paper. Measure and record the radius length along each of the radii previously drawn.

5. Graph the measurements, using the angle as the *x* axis and the radius as the *y* axis on the graph paper. Using the resulting graph, try to fit the results into an equation. Test the equations by graphing them in the same fashion, or by graphing them as polar equations and comparing the results to the actual spiral of the wave.

6. Write a BASIC program with the Microsoft QuickBASIC software that draws polar spirals, with user-definable constants. Include logarithmic spirals as an option. Using this program, adjust the constants to determine the equation that most closely matches that of the spiral of the wave.

7. Express the best equation in logarithmic form $ln(r) = K\theta$ and $r = C^{\theta}$, where k and c are constants.

8. Through observation and experimentation, determine the angular rotations between the three spirals.

RESULTS

1. Describe your observations when folding with a different number of divisions and with an uneven number of divisions. What were the

results? Was the basic shape of the spiral changed or unchanged? Why?

2. What were the three equations for the angles between secants? Were they the same for all three spirals? Why or why not? Were you able to determine a polar equation from your results? If so, did it show any connection to the Golden Mean?

3. What did the measurements show about the relationship between angle and radius? What type of equation seems to best approximate the measurements? Was there any noticeable relationship to the Golden Mean? What are the disadvantages of using this method?

4. Were you able to find an equation that produced a spiral similar to those in "The Wave"? What was the final result? Is there any relationship to the Golden Mean? Can you prove it?

5. What were the rotations between the inner and outer spirals? How could you see this without drawing the graphs? What were the rotations between the outer and middle spirals?

6. What other observations or conclusions can you make? Are there any additional connections to the Golden Mean?

What Substance Is Most Effective in Preventing the Breeding of Bacteria in Water Beds?

PURPOSE

To determine whether bacteria are present inside water beds and whether commercial water bed conditioners or other disinfectants are effective in counteracting any organisms that may live inside.

MATERIALS NEEDED

- water specimens from new and used water beds
- sterile applicators
- petri dishes: tryptic soy agar (TSA) with 5% sheep blood and MacConkey
- incubator
- API biochemical test manual
- several brands water bed conditioner
- household disinfectants
- warm tap water
- sterile cups
- sterile filter paper disks

EXPERIMENT

Specimens will be taken from both new and used water beds. These samples will be streaked individually onto separate TSA petri dishes, incubated, and observed for bacteria. If present, the bacteria will then be streaked onto MacConkey petri dishes, incubated, and observed for the presence of gram-negative bacteria which will then be identified through the use of an API biochemical test. Following this step, the water bed specimens will be streaked again onto another group of TSA petri dishes, while sterile filter paper disks that have each been dipped into a different type of water bed conditioner and disinfectant will be placed on top of the dishes. The petri dishes will be incubated for 48 hours and the conditioners' effectiveness will be assessed.

PROCEDURE

1. Collect water samples from inside several water beds and label the specimens to indicate the age and make of each bed they were taken from. Streak a portion of each onto a separate TSA petri dish, cover, label, and incubate them for 48 hours to determine if and how much bacteria are present. Compare and record your observations. If bacteria are present, streak the bacteria from each particular dish onto a corresponding MacConkey dish to determine the presence of gram-negative bacteria which will be identified by an API test. API test instructions can be found in an API biochemical test manual.

2. Streak another portion of the specimen onto more TSA petri dishes. Prepare a solution of each brand of water bed conditioner and disinfectant by diluting them in a solution of 1 part chemical to 5 parts water in sterile cups. Next, dip each of several sterile filter paper disks into a separate solution and place them individually on top of separate dishes (leave one dish untreated to serve as the control). Cover each dish and incubate for 48 hours.

3. Remove the filter paper disks to see if the conditioners and household disinfectants had any effect in reducing or eliminating the amount of bacteria that was present. This can be observed by measuring the clear zones found within the area in which the disks were placed on the petri dishes.

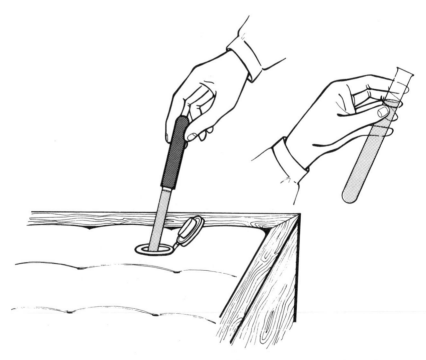

Remove water samples from each water bed with a large dropper and put them into individual test tubes.

RESULTS

1. What types of bacteria were found in the water beds? Were any pathogenic?

2. Did the age or make of the water beds influence the amount and type of bacteria found in them, or were all the beds consistent?

3. Was the amount of bacteria present in the petri dishes reduced or eliminated as a result of the treated filter paper disks?

4. Of all the chemicals used, which would be the best to keep a water bed free of organisms? (This can be determined by measuring the area of the clear zones on the petri dishes once the disks are removed.)

32

How Can the Amount of Bacteria Found on Kitchen Sponges and Dishrags Be Reduced?

PURPOSE

To discover which of several materials used to clean kitchen utensils with, and the location this material is kept in; will harbor the most bacteria. To determine the measures that would need to be taken in order to reduce most of bacteria found in the materials after use.

MATERIALS NEEDED

- 2 kitchen sponges
- 2 dishrags
- 2 dish mops
- 18 sterile cotton swabs
- 18 petri dishes: tryptic soy agar (TSA) with 5% sheep blood
- 18 plastic bags
- camera
- 18 soiled eating utensils
- soapy water
- boiled water

EXPERIMENT

A variety of materials commonly used to wash eating utensils will be tested to see the amounts of bacteria each will contain after use. Several methods of reducing this bacteria before and after use will be tried and compared for effectiveness. The locations in which utensils are kept will also be tested to see which environment is ideal for reducing the amount of bacteria that can be acquired by the materials.

124

PROCEDURE

1. Select two sponges, dishrags, and dish mops that have never been used and label a petri dish for each one of them. Next, rub a moistened sterile cotton swab across each and streak it onto its marked petri dish. Cover the petri dishes and put them into plastic bags at room temperature for 24 hours and then photograph each dish.

2. Divide the soiled utensils into six groups (each group will be washed with a different material). Proceed to wash one group of the utensils with one of the sponges. Then, rinse the sponge with soapy tap water, squeeze it out, and rub another sterile cotton swab across its surface. Streak the cotton swab onto its labeled petri dish, and cover. Then, wash another group of dirty utensils with the other sponge, rinse that sponge with boiled water, and squeeze it out. Rub a cotton swab over its surface, streak it onto another marked petri dish, and cover. Place both dishes into plastic bags at room temperature and photograph each after 24 hours.

3. Repeat Step 2 with the remaining groups of utensils and dishwashing materials. Then, analyze each photograph of the petri dishes to determine which material provided the best environment for bacterial growth and which rinsing method eliminated or counteracted the proliferation of bacteria.

4. For the second part of the experiment, place each material in a separate area of your kitchen immediately after being used in the first part of the experiment. (Possible locations include: underneath a sink, on the back of a stove top, on a counter top, and on the back corner of a sink top). Allow the materials to stay in their locations for 24–48 hours and then streak each onto a specially marked petri dish. Again, cover the dishes and put them into plastic bags at room temperature. Observe your results.

RESULTS

1. Did any of the dishwashing implements contain any bacterial contamination before they were used?

2. Which material provided the best environment for the bacteria to grow?

3. Which rinsing method appeared to be the most effective in either eliminating or reducing the amount of bacteria present after washing?

4. Did the storage of the sponges, dish mops, or dishrags have any influence on the amount of bacteria present in the materials 24–48 hours after use?

5. What do your results imply about the cleanliness of utensils even after they are washed?

33

What Type of Breath Freshener Has the Most Antibacterial Effects?

PURPOSE

To determine which of several substances that have been used to combat bad breath over the past 100 years is most effective in combatting bacteria.

MATERIALS NEEDED

- ◆ 7 sterile applicators
- ◆ 7 petri dishes: tryptic soy agar (TSA) with 5% sheep blood
- ◆ ¼ cup of mouthwash
- ◆ 6 plastic cups
- ◆ 1 breath mint
- ◆ 1 teaspoon nutmeg
- ◆ 1 teaspoon cinnamon
- ◆ 1 teaspoon ground parsley
- ◆ 1 teaspoon baking soda
- ◆ sterile water
- ◆ forceps
- ◆ 6 sterile filter paper disks
- ◆ incubator

EXPERIMENT

Seven oral bacteria samples from the same person will be streaked onto the seven petri dishes. Six of the petri dishes will be covered individually with a filter paper disk soaked in a different solution of the breath fresheners. The seventh dish, the control, will not be covered with a disk. The dishes will be incubated for a period of 24 hours and observations will be made to see which substance had the most antibacterial effect.

126

PROCEDURE

1. With a sterile applicator, swab the inside of your mouth and streak a petri dish. Repeat for all seven dishes.

2. Prepare a concentrated solution of the breath fresheners by dissolving each into ½ cup of water.

3. With forceps, dip a sterile filter paper disk into each solution and place one filter on top of the bacteria in each petri dish, except for the seventh dish, which will serve as the control.

4. Cover and incubate each dish for 24 hours and observe the conditions in each of the seven petri dishes.

RESULTS

1. Did the breath fresheners have any effect in reducing or eliminating the amount of oral bacteria that was present in the control petri dish?

2. Which substance seemed to have had the most effect? What element in this substance was probably responsible for this effect?

3. Does the substance that reduced or eliminated the most bacteria actually work as well as a breath freshener?

34

An Analysis of the Bacteria and Heavy Metal Content in Sewage Before and After Treatment at a Sewage Plant

PURPOSE

To analyze and compare the bacteria and heavy metal content in sewage from several sewage plants before treatment, and to determine what effects the treatment had on the sewage by analyzing and comparing its bacterial and heavy metal contents.

MATERIALS NEEDED

- samples of untreated raw sewage and effluent from several treatment plants
- samples of sewage and effluent after treatment
- sterile wood applicator sticks
- petri dishes: tryptic soy agar (TSA) with 5% sheep blood, colistin nalidixic acid (CNA), and MacConkey

- incubator
- API biochemical test manual
- sterile test tubes
- buffer reagent
- dithizone solution

EXPERIMENT

Both raw and treated samples of the same type of sewage will be obtained from several sewage treatment plants. TSA petri dishes will first be used to determine the amount of bacteria present in the raw sewage. Then, CNA petri dishes which grow only gram-positive bacteria and MacConkey petri dishes which grow only gram-negative bacteria, will be used. Second, API tests will then be administered to identify the types of gram-negative bacteria present. Finally, the presence of heavy metals will be noted with the use of buffer and dithizone solution reagents. The experiment will then be repeated with the sewage samples after treatment.

PROCEDURE

1. Obtain untreated samples of sewage from several plants.

2. Place sterile wooden applicators into each sample, streak them onto individual TSA petri dishes, and incubate them for 48 hours. After incubation, analyze the dishes to record the amount of bacteria present. Be sure to label each dish as to the location it came from. This information will be used to compare the treated samples.

3. Repeat Step 1 using CNA petri dishes, which grow only gram-positive bacteria, and MacConkey dishes, which grow only gram-negative bacteria. Incubate the dishes for 48 hours and then record the amount of bacterial growth in all the dishes.

4. Conduct the API tests (you will need to follow the instructions found in an API manual) to identify the types of gram-negative bacteria present in the MacConkey dishes.

5. Determine the amount of heavy metals, if any, that are present within the untreated sewage samples. Put 10 ml of each sample's effluent into individual test tubes and add 0.1 grams of the buffer reagent and 1.6 ml of the dithizone reagent to each and shake vigorously. A noticeable change in the color of the effluents will indicate the presence of heavy metals.

6. Repeat Steps 2–6 with the treated sewage samples from the same plants. Record, analyze, and compare your results to the untreated samples to see if the bacteria or heavy metal content has decreased.

RESULTS

1. Compare the types of bacteria found at each site. What type of bacteria was the most common among the different plants?

2. Was any of the bacteria found to be pathogenic?

3. Were heavy metals found in the effluent of any sewage samples? What did this indicate about the types of industries that use the particular sewage plant from which the samples came?

4. Did the treatment of the sewage decrease or alter the state of the bacteria and/or the heavy metals?

35 Are Your Clams Safe to Eat?

PURPOSE

To determine if clams purchased fresh from local fish markets—as opposed to those which have gone through a depuration process at a purification plant—are safe enough to eat.

MATERIALS NEEDED

- 60 clams from fish markets in 10 different regions
- alcohol or boiling water for sterilization
- sterile pan
- sterile knife
- blender
- sterile applicators
- petri dishes: tryptic soy agar (TSA) with 5% sheep blood
- incubator
- sterile jars
- photographed petri dishes of depured clams (as a control)

EXPERIMENT

Clams from different geographical areas that have not been purified will be bacteria-tested in both a raw and cooked state to observe and compare the fecal counts between the different locations to those of photographed petri dishes of purified clams.

PROCEDURE

1. Obtain six clams each from about 10 fish markets in different geographical areas. Be sure to label the areas from which each group came.

Brian Curtin bacteria-tested raw and depurified clams from different geographical areas to determine if they were safe to eat.

2. Sterilize all equipment with alcohol and/or boiling water.

3. Take three clams of one group and steam them in a sterile pan for five minutes. Then, open them with a sterile knife and put their contents together in a blender for 90 seconds.

4. Using a sterile applicator, streak the blend onto a petri dish and incubate for 24 hours.

5. Repeat the blending and streaking procedure using the remaining three clams from the group. Do not steam them.

6. Repeat Steps 3–5 with clams from the other geographical groups.

7. Compare the results from each group as a whole to the (control) photographed petri dishes of both the raw and steamed clams that had gone through the depuration process of a purification plant.

8. Identify the types of bacteria persent and the levels at which they can be safely consumed.

RESULTS

1. How does the bacteria count of the raw clams compare to that of the steamed clams? Did steaming in fact kill the bacteria? Are the raw clams safe to eat?

2. How did the bacteria count of the clams compare from market to market? From market to control?

3. Was all the bacteria that was found in the clams harmful?

36 Footwear versus Bacteria

PURPOSE

To determine whether footwear provides an environment for the growth of bacteria, and if so, to discover which type of footwear grows the most bacteria.

MATERIALS NEEDED

- 10 different types of footwear
- sterile applicators
- sterile water
- petri dishes: tryptic soy agar (TSA) with 5% sheep blood, colistin nalidixic acid (CNA), and MacConkey
- incubator
- graph paper

EXPERIMENT

A variety of footwear from 10 different people will be used for the first part of the experiment to determine whether significant amounts of bacteria grew during the time they were worn. TSA petri dishes will be used. For the second part of the experiment, the type of bacteria that grew most abundantly (gram-positive or gram-negative) will be identified, and the kind of footwear that provided the most ideal conditions for its growth will be determined. This will be done with CNA petri dishes and MacConkey petri dishes.

PROCEDURE

1. Swab the inside of each shoe or sneaker, before it is to be worn, with a sterile applicator moistened with the sterile water. Streak a separate TSA petri dish with each applicator. Incubate the petri dishes for 48 hours. After incubation, analyze the dishes to determine the amount of bacterial growth. Be sure to label the names of the individuals who will wear those particular shoes. This procedure will serve as a control for the experiment.

2. After the shoes and sneakers have been worn for 5 hours, swab the inside of each with the sterile applicators moistened with the sterile water. Then streak each applicator on individual TSA petri dishes. Again, be sure to label the dishes. Incubate the petri dishes for 48 hours and observe them.

3. After incubating the experimental petri dishes, compare them with their corresponding control petri dishes to see whether there were substantial increases in the amount of bacteria present.

4. Swab the inside of the same 10 shoes with the moist sterile applicators and streak each on CNA petri dishes, which grow only gram-positive bacteria and on MacConkey petri dishes, which grow only gram-negative bacteria. Again, be sure to label the dishes. Then, incubate the dishes for 48 hours. After incubation, compare the bacterial growth between all the dishes and photograph each dish.

5. Prepare tables to graph the data. For Part 1, record the amount of bacteria grown as small, medium, or large for each type of footwear. For Part 2, record the growth found in each petri dish for each individual type of footwear.

Swab the inside of a shoe or sneaker with a sterile applicator, before and after it has been worn for 5 hours. Streak the applicator onto TSA, CNA, and MacConkey petri dishes.

133

RESULTS

1. Did the use of the footwear for the 5-hour period increase the amount of bacteria present before the experiment?

2. Which type of footwear provided the best environment for the growth of bacteria?

3. Was there any type of footwear that grew little or no bacteria?

4. What type of bacteria grew more abundantly—gram-negative or gram-positive? What does this tell you about the type of bacteria present?

5. What type of footwear seems to be the best to wear? The worst?

37 The P-Trap: A Bacteria Cauldron

PURPOSE

To investigate the P-Trap (the "U"-shaped pipe located underneath a sink) in various households to determine:

1. Whether P-Traps are vehicles conducive for the growth of bacteria.

2. Whether such bacteria could be harmful to humans.

3. What products could be used to prevent the growth of bacteria at such sites.

MATERIALS NEEDED

- disinfectant spray
- sterile inoculating loop
- matches
- 20 different household sink P-Traps
- petri dishes: tryptic soy agar (TSA) with 5% sheep blood and MacConkey
- incubator
- Gram's stain test materials: (glass slides, Bunsen burner, crystal violet solution, tap wa-ter, iodine solution, 95% ethanol, safranin, microscope with oil-immersion lens)
- sterile filter paper discs
- forceps
- variety of liquid and solid household cleaning products
- API biochemical test manual

An International Science and Engineering Fair Project

Katherine Orzel was a finalist at the International Science and Engineering Fair in Fort Worth, Texas, in 1986, and continued her research on the same topic, which brought her finalist honors again at the ISEF in Knoxville, Tennessee, in 1988.

PROCEDURE

Part I

1. Wash hands and work area with a disinfectant spray.
2. Sterilize the inoculating loop by passing it through a match flame.
3. Remove the sink drain plug.
4. Lower the sterile inoculating loop into the sink for 15 seconds.
5. Streak the wet applicator onto a TSA petri dish.
6. Cover, invert and place the petri dish in an incubator for 48 hours.
7. Wash hands and work area again with disinfectant spray.
8. Wait 48 hours. Remove the petri dish from the incubator, observe the bacterial growth, and make a Gram's stain from the culture to determine whether the bacteria is gram-positive or gram-negative. This can be done by smearing a colony of bacteria from the petri dish onto a sterile glass slide. Allow the slide to dry and then warm it by passing it over the flame of a Bunsen burner.
9. Then flood the smear with crystal violet solution and allow it to stand for one minute. Next, wash the smear with tap water, flood it with iodine solution, and allow it to stand for one minute.

10. Wash the smear again and decolorize it with 95% ethanol until the dye does not run off the smear. Wash the smear again and then counterstain it with safranine for about 30 seconds. Finally, wash it again and allow it to dry.

11. Examine the slide under the oil immersion lens of a microscope. Gram-positive organisms will be blue, and gram-negative organisms will be red.

12. Repeat Steps 1–11 with samples from 19 other P-Traps.

Part II

1. Streak the petri dishes with water cultures from 20 different P-Traps in household sinks.

2. Dip sterile filter paper disks with forceps into dilutions of the various household cleaning substances and place on the streaked petri dishes.

3. Incubate these petri dishes for 48 hours and observe the results.

4. Repeat the experiment with the various cleaning substances that appear to be the most effective in counteracting the bacteria, by cleaning the P-Traps with them.

5. Take cultures from the traps, streak them onto petri dishes, and incubate them. Then, take more cultures from the same P-Traps 18 hours later, streak them onto TSA and MacConkey petri dishes and incubate them for 48 hours.

6. Observe the conditions of all the petri dishes and make a Gram's stain (explained in steps 8–11).

7. Finally, using an API manual, do an API biochemical test on the MacConkey dishes to identify the type of gram-negative bacteria present in them.

RESULTS

1. Is the P-Trap conducive for the growth of bacteria?

2. Does the type of detergent used affect the growth of the bacteria?

3. Does the length of time that the water stands in the P-Trap make any difference in the bacterial growth?

4. What is the best substance to use to clean out the P-Trap?

5. Was any of the bacteria found to be pathogenic?

38

The P-Trap: A Continuing Dilemma

Note: This project is a continuing study of Project 37: "The P-Trap: A Bacteria Cauldron."

PURPOSE

The purpose of the second phase of this study is:

1. To compare water from selected P-Traps that were investigated previously with samples from the same sites today.
2. To further identify organisms found in the traps.
3. To test the water for the presence of anaerobic bacteria.
4. To design a mechanism to control the growth of pollutant substances.

MATERIALS NEEDED

- disinfectant spray
- water samples from 20 different P-Traps
- petri dishes: MacConkey and tryptic soy agar (TSA) with 5% sheep blood
- sterile inoculating loop
- Gram's stain materials
- BBL GasPaks

- incubator
- API tests
- candle jar
- reverse camp test
- dilution plate test (instructions can be found in a microbiological text)

An International Science and Engineering Fair Project

PROCEDURE

1. Disinfect hands and work area with disinfectant spray.

2. Obtain water from the P-Trap, streak it onto a petri dish with an inoculating loop, and incubate it for 48 hours. Repeat this same procedure, using water from five other sites that were tested previously in Project 37: "The P-Trap: A Bacteria Cauldron."

3. Do Gram's stains on all six petri dishes (see Steps 1–11 in Project 37).

4. Compare the results with the previous findings.

5. Streak two petri dishes with water from a new site. Incubate one in a BBL GasPak and the other in a regular incubator. After 48 hours, take a culture from the aerobic dish (the dish placed in the regular incubator), subculture it onto a MacConkey dish and incubate it for 18 hours. Observe and complete Gram's stains and API tests. Repeat this procedure using the water from a different P-Trap.

A student can always participate at another science fair with the same topic if he or she has continued research on it or expanded its objective.

6. Streak two petri dishes with water from a P-Trap and incubate them, one in a candle jar and one in a GasPak for 48 hours. Divide two more petri dishes into four quadrants each and subculture them with bacteria colonies from the anaerobic petri dish (GasPak) and incubate them for 48 hours. Do Gram's stains and API tests and observe. Repeat this procedure using P-Trap water from 12 other sites.

7. At this point, only facultative anaerobes (organisms which can be grown with or without oxygen) have been isolated from the P-Trap. Place TSA petri dishes into GasPaks, seal them and leave at room temperature for 24 hours to remove the oxygen from the petri dishes.

8. Carry out four additional experiments using the same procedure as in Step 5, except that oxygen-free petri dishes should be used to isolate the anaerobic bacteria.

9. Use reverse camp tests to identify the anaerobic bacteria from the petri dishes placed in the GasPak.

10. Use the dilution plate test to determine the number of bacterial colonies, both aerobic and anaerobic, present in the P-Traps.

11. Finally, review all of the experiments. Review the piping system and its impact on humans and the environment. Determine what could be done to solve this dilemma, that is, a solution to keep the P-Trap bacteria-free.

RESULTS

1. Is there any difference in the amount of debris found in the P-Trap with that found previously?

2. How many different types of aerobic bacteria could be isolated from the trap?

3. What is the difference between facultative and obligate anaerobic bacteria?

4. Is there any correlation between the bacteria found in the P-Trap and people who use the sink?

5. How long can bacteria remain dormant in the stagnant water of an unused P-Trap?

6. How much bacteria, aerobic and anaerobic, is found in a P-Trap?

7. Can some type of mechanism be used in place of the P-Trap, or can some device be used to keep the P-Trap bacteria-free?

39

Improving the Antibacterial Effects of Garlic

PURPOSE

To determine whether the antibacterial ability of a garlic plant can be increased by foliar applications of a garlic extract solution.

MATERIALS NEEDED

- garlic bulb
- 20 plant containers
- all purpose soil (enough to fill 20 plant containers)
- sterile distilled water
- food processor
- cheesecloth
- 3 sterile glass containers
- fine mist atomizer
- *Esherichia coli* bacteria culture
- sterile swabs
- tryptic soy agar plate with 5% sheep blood
- knife or scissors
- tap water (warm)
- isopropyl rubbing alcohol
- dropper
- sterilized forceps
- sterile filter paper disks
- incubator

EXPERIMENT

Two groups of garlic plants will be grown: experimental and control. The experimental plants will have the garlic extract added to their leaves by a foliar spray, while the control group will be sprayed only with water. The treated leaves will then be pulverized into a solution whose antibacterial effects will be analyzed when applied to a culture of bacteria.

An International Science and Engineering Fair Project

PROCEDURE

Part I

Plant three series of garlic plants as follows:

1. From one bulb of garlic obtain 20 cloves of garlic (to insure genetic similarity) and plant one clove into each of 20 plant containers containing potting soil. Add equal amounts of sterile water to each container, watering plants as necessary.

2. Label 10 plants "Experimental" and 10 "Control" (from each series).

3. Grow plants for 10 days (until leaves are present and growth is about 6 inches in height).

1. Filter the pulverized garlic leaves through a cheesecloth into a jar and add three drops of sterile distilled water. This will be done with both the experimental and control leaves.

2. Transfer the E. coli bacteria to the tryptic soy agar plate with sterile swabs.

3. Soak the sterile filter paper disks in both the experimental and control filtered leaf extracts.

4. Place two filter disks that were soaked in the experimental plant leaf extract onto two sections of the tryptic soy agar plate and then place the control disks onto the two other sections for the zone of inhibition study.

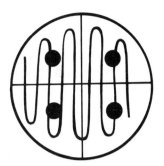

Part II

Prepare the garlic extract solution:

1. Obtain the cloves from one bulb of garlic and peel them.
2. Pulverize the cloves in a food processor until they are nearly liquefied.
3. Filter the extract by squeezing as much of the liquid portion as possible through cheesecloth into a glass container.
4. Prepare a one-to-one ratio of garlic extract to distilled water for the garlic spray solution.
5. Fill the fine mist atomizer with the garlic solution. Spray each of the experimental plants with two sprays of the solution and continue to do the same every other day.
6. Fill the fine mist atomizer with distilled water. Spray each of the control plants with two sprays of the water and continue to do the same every other day.

Part III

Prepare the culture dishes:

1. Transfer the *Escherichia coli* bacteria to the tryptic soy agar plate with 5% sheep blood with a sterile swab.
2. Mark the bottom of the plate into four equal pie-shaped areas. Label two sections "Experimental" (A and B) and two "Control" (A and B).

Part IV

Prepare the test materials from each garlic plant:

1. Cut off the green leaves above the cloves.
2. Thoroughly wash the plant under warm running water to remove any residues of sprayed materials.

3. Pulverize the leaves of all the experimental plants in an alcohol sterilized food processor and with the dropper add three drops of sterile distilled water. Repeat with the control plants. (Keep the mixtures in sterile containers until they will be used for the zone of inhibition study.)

Part V

Prepare the petri plates for the zone of inhibition study:

1. Soak sterile filter paper disks in the garlic test solution made from the leaves of each garlic plant (as described in Part II).
2. With the forceps place two filter disks soaked in the experimental plant mixture onto the two experimental pie sections of the plate. Place two filter disks soaked in the control plant mixture onto the two control sections of the plate.
3. Incubate the plate for 24 hours at 37° Celsius. Measure the diameter of the zones of inhibition in millimeters and record your data.

RESULTS

1. Compare the diameters of the zones of inhibition in the control and experimental groups. Did they differ? How much of a variance existed between the two groups? Which of the two groups had the largest diameters?
2. Which group showed the greatest antibacterial effect? Did the garlic spray affect the antibacterial ability of the garlic plant?

40

Does the Period of Motion of a Pendulum Depend on Its Weight, Amplitude, or Length?

PURPOSE

To determine if changes in the weight, amplitude, or length affect the period of motion of a pendulum.

MATERIALS NEEDED

To construct the pendulum frame:

- 7 pieces of 2″ × 1″ wood (5 pieces 2 feet long for the base and top panel and 2 pieces 3 feet long for the upright sides of the frame)
- 6 small metal angles, screws, and/or nails

To construct the pendulum:

- screw hook
- fishing weights (minimum 30 units of 1 ounce = 0.028 kilogram each)

- small plastic bottle with cap
- 1 thin fishing line (minimum of 10 feet)

To measure the variables:

- ruler
- protractor
- kitchen balance
- stopwatch that can measure to 1/100 of a second

EXPERIMENT

A simple pendulum will be constructed and set into motion several times, with changes made in its variables of weight, length, and angles of release. The average period will be computed, together with its standard deviation for each experimental run.

PROCEDURE

1. Assemble the pendulum frame using the diagram as a reference. Be sure to attach the screw hook to the center of the upper wood frame. Attach protractor as shown. Weigh (W) a random number of fishing weights, put them into the small plastic bottle, and attach the cap. Cut a length (L) of the fishing line and tie one end to the plastic bottle cap and the other to the hook. At this point the pendulum is ready to be set into motion.

2. Bring the bottle to an amplitude of (A) degrees (as indicated by the protractor) from the vertical, and release the pendulum. Time the period of motion (P) with a stopwatch that can measure to 1/100th of a second. This is the time between two successive passes of the pendulum through the maximum amplitude. Repeat this procedure (N) times (e.g., 10 times) to get consistent results.

3. Compute the average time period (T) and the standard deviation (S):

$$T = \Sigma\ P/N$$
$$S = \sqrt{\Sigma\ (P-T)^2/N}$$

where $P\ (i = 1, 2, \ldots n)$ are the individual measured periods.

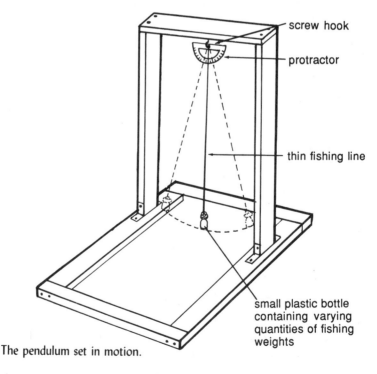

The pendulum set in motion.

4. Repeat steps 2 and 3 with several different values for the three independent variables of length (L), weight (W) and amplitude (A). Select three to five different lengths from a minimum of about 2 feet to the maximum allowed by the height of your pendulum. Select two or three different weights totaling from about 10 to 30 oz. Two or three different amplitudes can also be used in the range of 10 to 30 degrees. (Each run is, of course, characterized by the values of the three independent variables.)

RESULTS

1. Compare the experimental results from all the trial runs with different weights. Did most of the experimental results stay close to the standard deviation (S) of the average period (T)?

2. If not, were the differences significant? Judging from your results, do you believe that the period of motion was dependent upon the weight, amplitude, or length of the pendulum?

41 Are Composites of Wood Stronger than Solid Wood?

PURPOSE

To determine if a wood composite, which is made of a combination of materials that have been saturated with a resin or glue, has a greater torsional resistance (twisting) and drop resistance (bending) than a comparable piece of solid wood.

MATERIALS NEEDED

Testing apparatus:

- panel of wood 2.5′ × 2′ (test platform)
- metal workshop horse with clamps (to support test bars)
- assorted screws, nuts, and bolts (to fasten the metal workshop horse to the test platform)
- round disk (calibrated in degrees) with attached 4-inch arm

- wire fishing line
- spring scale
- several ¼-pound lead fishing weights

Test bars:

- 10 composite bars (1 foot long by ⅜-inch square)
- 10 composite bars (1 foot long by ⅜-inch square)

EXPERIMENT I: TORSIONAL RESISTANCE (TWISTING)

Force will be applied to the short wire line from the 4-inch arm at a setting of 4 pounds on the attached spring scale. This will move the arrow on the 4-inch arm to measure the degree of twist on the round disk through which the test sample passes (see diagram). This will be done to both the composite and solid test bars.

PROCEDURE I

1. Set up the test platform as it is shown in the diagram for the twisting test. In general, this means that a test bar will be held between two clamps supported by a metal workshop horse. One end of the test bar will pass through a rotating round disk that will measure the arc (in degrees) of twist on the test bar. Attached to the side of the round disk will be a 4-inch arm with a hooked wire line that will suspend a spring scale. Various lead fishing weights will be hooked onto the spring scale which will cause the 4-inch arm to move downward while rotating the round disk. This will cause the test bar to twist.

2. Place the composite bar in the holding apparatus.

3. Attach the spring scale to the 4-inch lever arm. This will automatically place a factor of 4:1 on the scale.

4. Apply force to the wire line by adding weights to the spring scale at a predetermined weight of 4 pounds. Now, measure the arc of twist on the scaled round disk.

5. Continue to increase force at increments of one pound, and measure the arc of twist until the composite wood bar snaps.

6. Remove the composite bar and repeat Steps 2–5 with the normal solid wood bar.

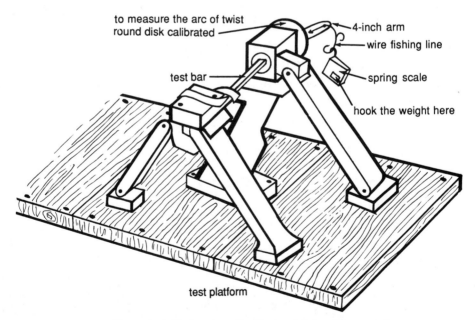

The test platform set up for the torsional resistance test.

EXPERIMENT 2: DROP RESISTANCE (BENDING)

The sample will be held at one end and a predetermined amount of weight will be applied in a downward direction at the opposite end, by means of an attached spring scale. The amount of drop resistance will be measured in thousandths of an inch.

PROCEDURE 2

1. Set up the test platform for the drop resistance test. This can be done by removing the side of the horse with the attached round disk and 4-inch arm.
2. Place a composite bar in the remaining holding apparatus and attach the wire line to the opposite end of the bar.
3. Hook the spring scale to the wire line.
4. Apply force through the spring scale at a predetermined weight setting, and measure the drop of the bar.
5. Continue to increase the force by ¼-pound increments and measure the drop of the bar until the composite wood bar snaps.
6. Remove the composite bar and repeat Steps 2–5 with the normal solid wood bar.

RESULTS

1. Compare the amounts of force that were needed to move each bar one degree mark when torsional resistance was tested. Which bar proved to be more resistant?
2. Which bar continued to show resistance even after the other had reached its peak resistance?
3. From your experimental results, which bar do you conclude is better at resisting force?

42

Which Angle of Attack Generates the Most Lift?

PURPOSE

To test four different angles of attack to determine which one generates the most lift.

MATERIALS NEEDED

- blowing fan
- small wind tunnel (2 feet in length, made of either ply-wood, balsa, or cardboard) (check with your supervisor for its construction)
- digital metric scale
- balsa wood testing platform
- easel clamp

- 4 balsa airfoil stands with 0-degree, 15-degree, 30-degree, and 50-degree angles cut into one end on each
- 4 balsa airfoils of the same di-mensions (glued to the angled face of the stand)
- stopwatch

EXPERIMENT

Each airfoil will be tested three times, and each test will run for 15 seconds. The 0-degree angle will serve as a control, and the other angles will act as variables. The highest force reading for each airfoil on the digital metric scale is to be recorded at the end of each test. The only variable in the experiment will be the difference in the angle of attack.

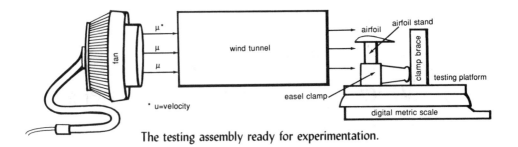

The testing assembly ready for experimentation.

PROCEDURE

1. Using the diagram as a general example, set up a wind tunnel testing assembly. Once the unit is set up, do not reposition the wind tunnel or testing platform. If these components are moved, the flow of air around the airfoil will change, and inaccurate results will be obtained.

2. Clamp the airfoil and the airfoil stand upright and place it on the balsa wood testing platform (refer to diagram). Then, place the testing assembly on the scale. The leading edge of the airfoil should be parallel to the edge of the wind tunnel's mouth.

3. Calibrate the scale.

4. Immediately after the scale has been calibrated, switch on the blowing fan. Simultaneously, begin timing the first 15-second test with the stopwatch. Then repeat this procedure for the second and third tests.

5. Record the highest force reading from the scale at the end of each of the three tests. Now repeat Steps 2–5 three times for each airfoil. Record the highest force reading of the three tests for each separate angle of attack.

6. Graph your results.

RESULTS

1. From your graphical results, which angle of attack generated the most lift?

2. Why did the angles generate the particular amounts of lift force that they did?

43

Polarization and Stress Analysis of Airplane Windows

PURPOSE

To discover the principles behind elliptically shaped airplane windows through a process of stress analysis called photoelasticity.

MATERIALS

- wood frame (5 cm × 5 cm × 66.5 cm)
- saw
- 6 5-centimeter squares of felt
- 2 polaroids with blue filters (polarizing filters)
- 2 ¼ wave plates (for clearer photographs)
- 2 small wooden blocks
- drill
- lamp with 200-watt light bulb (use a light bulb with a diffusion coating)
- 35-millimeter-lens, single reflex camera
- Lexon plastic (⅛ inch thick)
- glass cutter
- 2 metal rods
- 3 kilogram weight

EXPERIMENT

An instrument called a polariscope will be constructed to test the stresses that will occur in several sample windows. The shapes of the windows will be cut as holes in flat strips of plastic. These window models will be placed one at a time between crossed polaroids in the polariscope, while a 200-watt light bulb will shine inside. A 3-kg weight will be loaded onto the model inside the polariscope, and dark, bright bands will appear on the stressed plastic (simulated window). These colored bands, which are called isochromatic fringes, show the stress concentration on the plastic which represents the stresses that would be around a window. The place at which the fringes are closest together is where the stress concentration is the highest.

PROCEDURE

1. Build a wooden box for the frame of the polariscope. The two ends of the box are to be left open. Cut a slot at the top and bottom (see diagram). Line the slot at the top of the box with felt to prevent light from going around the crossed Polaroids. Line the base of the inner box with felt and leave 4 groove-sized gaps to support the Polaroids and wave plates. Then, fit the two Polaroids and wave plates into the slots. Align the two wooden blocks and drill one hole (for a rod) through both of them. Cover the lined slot at the top of the box with the blocks. Place the lamp and the camera at opposite ends.

2. Cut six pieces of Lexon plastic to 4.5 cm in width and 20.5 cm in length. Cut a hole in each piece with a glass cutter to represent an airplane window. Suggested shaped holes include: a circle, two circles (one above the other), circle with a smaller circle above and below, rectangle, diamond, and an elliptical shape (to serve as the control).

3. Drill two holes at the top and the bottom (where the metal rods will be placed) in each strip of plastic. The top rod will hold the model between the blocks in Step 1, which will allow the model to be lowered into the polariscope. The bottom rod will load the 3-kg weight onto the bottom of the model.

4. Slide one of the Lexon plastic window shapes through the top slot and insert the metal rods. Then hook on the 3-kg weight.

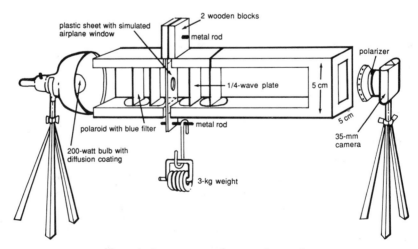

The polariscope set up for experimentation.

5. Take pictures of the isochromatic fringes, the color bands that appear near the plastic window opening, on the window model inside the polariscope. Different shutter speeds can be used if the pictures are under- or over-exposed. Otherwise, you may remove the camera and sketch the isochromatic fringes.

6. Repeat Steps 4 and 5 with the other window models and record your results.

RESULTS

1. Analyze the pictures of the models and their isochromatic fringes. Notice where the fringes are closest together. These areas are the points of highest stress concentration. Which areas on each model have high concentrations of stress? Which areas show the least? Why are the fringes arranged in this pattern?

2. Which models overall have the least area of high stress concentration? Why do these models have low stresses?

3. Which models are the easiest to produce? Which ones are more practical and easy to use?

4. Is the elliptical model indeed the best shape for an airplane window? If not, which model seems to be most effective?

5. What kinds of variances could arise in the process of this experiment? What are some possible solutions to eliminate them?

44

Shape and Viscous Effect

PURPOSE

Spherical objects falling in viscous fluid are known to obey Stokes' law. The purpose of this experiment is to determine if Stokes' law in the form of *drag × time = constant*, would apply to different clay shaped objects when dropped in viscous fluids, such as glycerin and corn syrup.

MATERIALS NEEDED

- plastic cup
- water
- balance scale (accuracy to 0.1 gram)
- 4 ounces glycerin
- 16 ounces corn syrup
- metric ruler
- metal molds (of several shapes)
- modeling clay
- lead fishing weights
- 100 milliliter graduated cylinder
- 500 milliliter graduated cylinder
- stopwatch (accuracy to 0.01 seconds)

EXPERIMENT

Four sets of differently shaped clay objects (sphere, cube, teardrop and a tetrahedron), all with the same volume but with different weights, will be dropped into a 100 ml graduated cylinder filled with glycerin and a 500-ml graduated cylinder filled with corn syrup. These objects will be timed with a stopwatch as each falls from the 100 ml to 20 ml line in glycerin and the 500 ml to 100 ml line in corn syrup. Then, the buoyancy, drag, and *drag × time* for each object will be calculated. The results will be checked to see if the *drag × time* was indeed equal to that of a sphere (*constant*).

PROCEDURE

1. Measure the density of the fluids by filling a cup with water, weighing it on the balance scale, and recording the weight. Do the same with the glycerin and corn syrup. Then, divide the weight of the glycerin into the weight of the water to obtain the specific gravity of the fluid. Do the same with the corn syrup. Next, multiply the specific gravity of 1 gm/cc (water's defined density) to get the density of the glycerin or corn syrup.

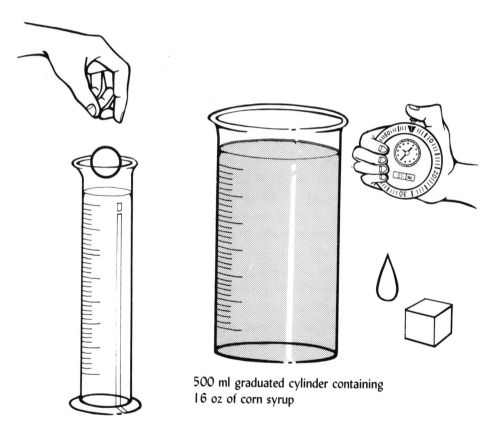

500 ml graduated cylinder containing 16 oz of corn syrup

100 ml graduated cylinder containing 4 oz of glycerin

Clay objects of various shapes will be timed as they fall through the viscous fluids to see if Stokes' law applies to them as it does to spheres.

157

2. Measure the height, width, and length of the metal molds and multiply all three measurements to get the volume of the mold. All clay objects to be made in the same mold will have the same volume.

3. Make the clay objects by pressing clay into the molds. Be sure that the molds are completely filled with the clay.

4. Make clay objects with lead fishing weights. Put clay in the molds and force one or two lead fishing weights in. Scrape off all excess clay pushed out (to maintain the same volume). All the space surrounding the lead fishing weight in the molds will be filled with clay. Make an equal number of objects with different weights, but of the same volume, for each shape.

5. Calculate the buoyancy, weight, and drag. The buoyancy is the object's volume (submerged in the fluid), multiplied by the fluid density. The weight of an object minus the buoyancy is the drag.

6. Control Test: Drop one of the objects into the 100-ml graduated cylinder of glycerin and start the stopwatch as soon as the ball hits the 100-ml line. Watch carefully as it glides through the glycerin. The moment it hits the 20-ml line, stop the stopwatch and record the time. Calculate the buoyancy, drag and the *drag × time* as the constant. Repeat for each object in glycerin and then in a 500-ml graduated cylinder of corn syrup to compare the falling times in each case, and to see if Stokes' law applies to the differently shaped objects.

RESULTS

1. What was the time "constant" of the balls dropped in glycerin?

2. How did the times of the cubes, teardrops, and tetrahedrons compare with those of the balls?

3. Which objects moved the slowest? The fastest? From your observations, can you say that drag is indeed related to the time it takes an object to fall from the top to the bottom of a graduated cylinder?

4. From your observations, would you say that Stokes' law applied to any of the different shaped objects?

45

What Would Happen to Climate, Weather Patterns, and Life Forms if the Earth Were Cubical?

PURPOSE

To theorize what effects a cube-shaped Earth would have on climate, weather patterns, and flora/fauna life.

MATERIALS NEEDED

Experiment 1

- ◆ 2 empty half-gallon milk cartons
- ◆ baking soda
- ◆ water
- ◆ white paper
- ◆ tape or glue
- ◆ world map
- ◆ metric ruler
- ◆ transparency film marker
- ◆ sheet transparency film
- ◆ overhead projector
- ◆ globe

Experiment 2

- ◆ soft ball (approx. 12 centimeter diameter)
- ◆ empty half-gallon milk carton
- ◆ 2 unsharpened pencils
- ◆ 2 thumb tacks
- ◆ modeling clay
- ◆ small squeeze bottle
- ◆ blue food coloring and water mixture

EXPERIMENT I

A grid will be drawn on a sheet of transparency film and projected onto an upright parallel globe to simulate the sun and to measure the concentrations of sunlight on various points of a spherical Earth. The same will be done with a cubical Earth and the results of each will be compared.

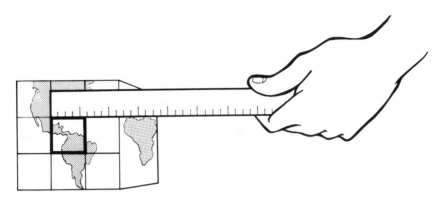

Beam the grid image onto the cubical Earth to simulate the angles at which sunlight would actually strike its surface. The light concentration should be the greatest at the center.

PROCEDURE I

1. Construct a cubical model of the Earth by cutting off the bottoms of two empty half-gallon milk containers and fitting them together. (The milk odor can be removed by soaking the cartons in a solution of baking soda and water for about 15 minutes.) Then cover the cube with white paper. Refer to the world map and draw the continents and oceans onto the cube as you think they might appear.

2. Use a metric ruler and the sheet transparency marker to make a grid on a clear sheet of the transparency film, with each square measuring 1 cc. Next, place the grid onto the overhead projector and beam the grid image onto an upright globe that is positioned parallel with the projector.

3. Locate a grid square beaming directly at a place near the 45 degrees latitude mark on the globe. Outline the shape directly on the globe. Repeat this procedure, locating a grid shape directly below the first, but at a place near the equator. Measure the length and width of each outlined shape, calculate its area, and note the concentration of light in each. This will simulate the angles at which sunlight strikes the Earth's spherical surface and the amount of light concentration at each angle.

4. Repeat Step 3 using the cubical Earth. For the 45-degree mark, measure one-fourth of the distance into the center of the light exposed side. For the equator, measure halfway into the center of the light exposed side.

RESULTS I

1. Compare the grid areas of the spherical Earth to those of the cubical Earth. Were there any differences in the way the simulated sunlight

was being concentrated on the different outlined points? If so, what do you think the overall climate of the cubical earth would be like?

EXPERIMENT 2

An approximately 12-cm half-sphere, made by cutting a lightweight ball in half, and a half-cube, made by cutting off the bottom of a half-gallon milk container, will be tacked loosely to the eraser tops of two different pencils so that they may spin freely. Then, each pencil unit will stand straight up in a lump of modeling clay. As their tops are spun, a steady stream of liquid will be squeezed over their surface. This procedure will theoretically compare and contrast some changes in the weather patterns that might occur if the earth were cubical.

PROCEDURE 2

1. Cut a half-sphere out of a small ball to be approximately 12 cm in diameter. Then cut out a half-cube from the bottom of an empty milk container. Tack the centers of each loosely to the eraser tops of two different pencils. Stand each pencil unit straight up in its

A half-sphere and a half-cube will be tacked loosely to the eraser tops of two pencils to simulate the Earth spinning on its axis. As each shape is spun, a steady stream of liquid will be squeezed over its surface to theoretically determine differences in weather patterns.

161

own lump of clay with the eraser side up. Test the half-sphere and half-cube to see that they spin freely without sliding down.

2. Fill half of a squeeze bottle with a mixture of water and blue food coloring. Then, spin the half-sphere while a friend squirts a steady stream of the blue dye from the center outward. Note the pattern made by the dye as it travels off the half-sphere.

3. Repeat Step 2 with the half-cube.

RESULTS 2

1. Was there any difference in the dye patterns between the two models? How much dye reached the equators of both models?

2. What kind of effects do you suppose the weather patterns of a cubical Earth would have on its flora and fauna?

46

The Effects of Hard and Soft Water Respiration from an Ultrasonic Humidifier on Mealworms

PURPOSE

To determine the effects that an ultrasonic humidifier (used to add moisture to dry rooms in winter) filled with either hard or soft water will have on mealworms.

MATERIALS NEEDED

- 6 cups of chopped food (corn flakes, fruits and vegetables)
- 3 square plastic containers ($8'' \times 8'' \times 6''$)
- 3 metal screens to serve as aerated covers
- 45 mealworm larvae
- scale (measures in grams)
- 2 ultrasonic humidifiers
- hard water
- soft water

EXPERIMENT

The mealworms will be divided into three equal groups. Group A will be placed under the vent of an ultrasonic humidifier that is filled with hard water. Group B will be placed under the vent of another humidifier that is filled with soft water. Group C will serve as the control and will not be subjected to any humidifier.

PROCEDURE

1. Prepare homes for the mealworms by chopping and crushing the food into small bits. Put an equal amount into each of the three plastic containers.

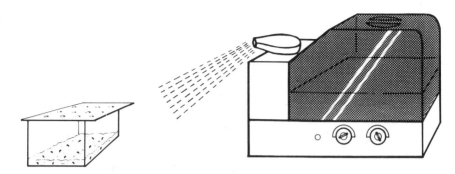

Place Group A under a humidifier emitting hard water and Group B under a humidifier emitting soft water, each for six hours per day for three days.

2. Divide the worms into three equal groups. Then, weigh each larvae in Group A in grams and average their weights to come up with the approximate average weight for Group A. Do the same for Groups B and C and be sure to record all your data.

3. Put each group into one of the three boxes and cover with the metal screens. Weigh each unit as a whole, record the figures, and cover each container with a metal screen.

4. Place Group A under the ultrasonic humidifier filled with hard water. Place Group B under the ultrasonic humidifier filled with soft water. Put Group C aside, free from the effects of any humidifier.

5. Turn on the humidifiers and leave them on for 6 hours.

6. Weigh each group as a whole. Then weigh the larvae from each group separately to obtain the average weight from each group.

7. Return the worms to their corresponding homes overnight. In the morning, place the "hard water" worms back under the humidifier with hard water and the "soft water" worms back under the humidifier with soft water. Leave the control worms alone.

8. Repeat Steps 5–6 for the second and third days, while noting the worms' behavior changes, activity levels, the rate at which they pupate into beetles, and the rate at which they die.

RESULTS

1. Compare the weights of the mealworms on days 1, 2 and 3. Was any group consistently losing weight or gaining weight in comparison to the other groups?

2. Were the experimental groups different from the control group?

3. Compare the overall behavior of the groups. Were there any significant differences between the two experimental groups? Which group developed the most (if at all)?

47

How Do Different Surfaces Affect the Distance Mealworms Travel in 2 Minutes?

PURPOSE

To chart and compare the distances mealworms travel on different surfaces.

MATERIALS NEEDED

◆ 10 surfaces of varying texture, such as sandpaper, cloth, paper towel, adhesive tape, flour, wood, cement, aluminum foil, rubber, and carpet

◆ 10 mealworms
◆ nail polish
◆ stopwatch

EXPERIMENT

Each of the 10 mealworms will be placed on various textured surfaces and timed for 2 minutes.

PROCEDURE

1. Obtain the different textured materials; each surface should be large enough for each mealworm to travel on.
2. Put a different color nail polish on the back of each mealworm to distinguish them.
3. Begin your experiment by making a mark at the center of one of the textured surfaces. Place a mealworm on this mark and set the stopwatch for 2 minutes to track its movement. Each time the worm changes direction, put a mark at that spot.

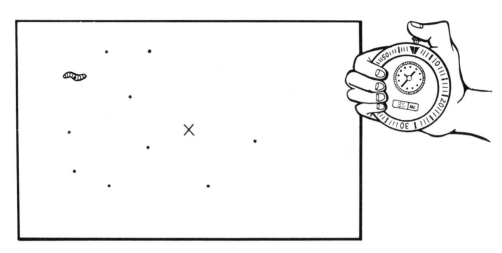

Place the mealworm at the center of the surface and set the stopwatch for 2 minutes. Mark a dot each time the worm moves in a different direction.

4. Take the mealworm off the surface, connect the marks using a ruler. Label and measure the line. Record the distance for that particular mealworm.

5. Repeat Steps 3 and 4 with each mealworm. Then, repeat all steps again with a new surface. Complete a total of 100 trials overall (10 per worm).

6. Graph the results for each worm and surface.

RESULTS

1. Compare the textures of each surface. Which types provided the most ideal conditions for locomotion? What does this tell you about the anatomy of the mealworm?

2. Were the mealworms consistent with each other on all the surfaces?

3. Do you think that the worms' surface locomotion was influenced by the habitats to which they are accustomed (for example, flour and grain cereals)?

Relaxing the Breathing Patterns of Newly Purchased Pet Fish So They May Adapt to a New Aquarium

PURPOSE

Because of the drastic environmental changes that occur as a fish moves from a pet-shop aquarium, to a plastic bag, to a home aquarium, the immune systems of many pet fish become weakened. Often this is because fish tanks are usually filled with tap water that is "bubbly" with oxygen gas. The fish often become sick from the shock and the high amount of oxygen in their bloodstreams. This experiment will determine if calcium carbonate (a compound that reduces excess gas), when applied to either fish food or fish-tank water, has any affect in dissolving the amount of oxygen gas present so that the fish may relax and adapt to their new homes more easily.

MATERIALS NEEDED

- 3 fish tanks (1 gallon each)
- clean tap water
- 3 fish from a pet shop (of the same breed)
- ½ teaspoon calcium carbonate
- pet fish food (for example, Tetramin brand)
- mortar and pestle

EXPERIMENT

One fish will receive the calcium carbonate in its food, while a second fish will be placed into a tank already containing the calcium carbonate (experimental groups). A third fish will be placed in a tank filled with new tap water and plain fish food (control). The fish will be monitored closely to count the number of gill movements per minute and their level of activity.

PROCEDURE

1. Fill each fish tank with an equal amount of clean tap water. Then, place all three "newly purchased" pet-shop fish into one of the tanks. For the first minute, record the rate at which the gills move and their levels of activity.

2. Stir $\frac{1}{4}$ teaspoon of calcium carbonate into the second tank. After it has dissolved into the water, place one of the fish into the tank and sprinkle in some plain fish food. Record its gill movements, activity, and appetite.

3. Place a different fish into the third tank. Prepare this fish's food by powdering a serving size of fish food with a mortar and pestle. Then mix $\frac{1}{4}$ teaspoon of calcium carbonate and several drops of water into the powdered food. Mix into the fish tank. Record the gill movements, level of activity, and appetite of this fish.

4. Allow the remaining fish to stay in the original tank. Feed it a meal of plain fish food only. Again, observe its gill movements, activity levels, and appetite.

5. Continue to monitor all the fish constantly for the first hour, or until every fish has completely adapted to its environment.

RESULTS

1. How did the fish react when they were originally placed together in the tap water tank? Did they appear different from the way they looked in the pet store? What were the number of gill movements per minute?

2. Did the calcium carbonate appear to have any effect in aiding the fish to adapt to their new environment? If so, which method of administering the compound appeared to be the best?

3. Which fish appeared to have adapted to its environment most quickly? What were its gill movements per minute after it had appeared to relax?

49

Can the Heartbeat of a Chicken Embryo Be Detected Without Breaking Its Eggshell?

PURPOSE

To see if it is possible to measure the early heartbeat of a chicken embryo without breaking its eggshell or disturbing the chick's development—as other methods have done in the past.

MATERIALS NEEDED

Note: It is recommended that this experiment be conducted under the supervision of a research scientist.

- Zygo Axiom 200 interfero-meter
- retroreflector and mount
- VAX computer by Digital Equipment Co.
- software package (such as Signal Processing Toolbox)

- 3 3-day-old incubated fertile chicken eggs
- 1 3-day-old dead chicken egg
- incubator

EXPERIMENT

The movement within an eggshell will be measured with a Zygo Axiom 200 interferometer (which sends a light from a laser through a beam splitter that splits the light beam in half). One half of that light will travel out to a fixed mirror and bounce back. The other half will travel out to a moveable mirror that is touching an egg, so that when its eggshell moves from the embryo's heartbeat, the mirror will also move. Therefore, the beam that will bounce off the moveable mirror will have its phase altered in such a way that when it returns back to the beam splitter (where it is combined with the other beam), constructive interference will result from the action of the waves joining in phases. Destructive interference will occur if the waves are out of phase. Then, the changes in the distance traveled by the beam going to the egg (in millionths of a millimeter) will be calculated from the patterns of light intensity. The experiment will be repeated on two more fertile embryos (to achieve consistent results) and on a dead embryo (as a control).

PROCEDURE

1. Obtain permission to work under the supervision of a research scientist, probably at a local university.

2. Set up the Zygo Axiom 200 interferometer, retroreflector and mount with your supervisor's assistance and connect the apparatus to a VAX computer that will record the data of the changing phases of the beam.

3. Obtain three fertile chicken eggs, together with a dead one, all of which are about 3 days old. Store them in an incubator. Place one

CAN THE HEARTBEAT OF A CHICKEN EMBRYO BE DETECTED WITHOUT BREAKING THE EGGSHELL?

Celeste Peterson found that the interferometer technique was extremely sensitive in picking up the tiny shell vibrations from the 3-day-old chicken embryos without breaking the chicks' eggshells or disturbing their progress.

egg at a time gently up against the moveable mirror on the retroreflector and expose it to the light beam for $1\frac{1}{2}$ minutes to collect data points. Repeat the procedure again when the eggs are 4 and 5 days old.

4. After the data points of the heartbeat frequencies have been sent to the VAX computer, they will be put onto a graph and analyzed as time versus displacement.

5. After experimentation, observe the condition of the eggshells for cracks, and carefully observe the eggs until they hatch, to see if this method has disturbed the chicks' progress in any way.

RESULTS

1. According to your recorded data, what were the average beats per second in each embryo's ventricle, atrium, and sinus venosus?

2. Were the beats per second less detectable as the embryo matured? Why do you suppose this occurred?

3. Did any of the eggshells crack as a result of experimentation? How long did it take before the eggs hatched? Were the chicks underdeveloped or harmed?

4. What other applications could this method be used for in studying the development of embryos inside shells?

171

50 ▷ Are Dogs Colorblind?

PURPOSE

To determine if dogs are in fact completely colorblind, as many people—including many veterinarians—believe.

MATERIALS NEEDED

- variety assorted colored construction paper
- camera
- 3 glass jars

- 1 dog—any age, breed, or sex, in good health
- dog biscuits or some other treat the dog likes

EXPERIMENT

Photographs of colored construction paper will be taken with black and white film to determine how colors appear under varying amounts of light. These pictures will simulate how shades of color will be perceived by a totally colorblind dog. A dog will be trained to continuously choose one distinctly different shaded jar (as it appears from the photos) from another distinctly different shaded jar. Once the dog is trained to choose the particular jar, the other jar will be replaced by a jar shaded similarly to the one the dog is trained to choose. The jar positions will be switched frequently to determine whether the dog can still recognize the shaded jar that it was trained to choose.

PROCEDURE

1. Take black and white photographs of an assortment of colored construction paper to determine which colors appear to have similar and dissimilar degrees of brightness and shade after the film is developed.

2. Cover two jars with differently colored construction paper that share a similar shade when photographed with black and white film. Cover the third jar with another color whose photographed shade is distinctly different from the other two shades.

3. For the first part of your experiment the dog will not be tested for colorblindness, but will be trained to select one of the similarly shaded jars from the differently shaded one. When the dog can consistently choose the correct jar, reward it with a treat.

4. For the second part of your experiment, replace the differently shaded jar with the second similarly shaded jar. The dog will need color vision to distinguish between the two jars, since with complete colorblindness the two colors would appear to be the same shade.

5. Switch the positions of the jars around frequently and test the dog 100 times. If the dog chooses correctly, continue to reward it to keep it interested. Chart the number of correct and incorrect responses made by the dog to the second part of your experiment.

After the dog has been trained to choose one jar of a particular degree of brightness and contrast as opposed to a darker shaded jar, color vision will then be necessary when the dog must choose the same jar as opposed to another one with a similar degree of brightness and contrast.

RESULTS

1. Was the dog able to distinguish between shades of brightness in the first part of your experiment?

2. Was the dog consistently correct, incorrect, or did it vary in its responses?

3. Was the dog able to distinguish between the similar shades in the second part of your experiment?

4. Was the dog consistently correct, incorrect, or did it vary in its responses?

5. If the dog was mostly correct, do you think that other variables may have accounted for its accuracy?

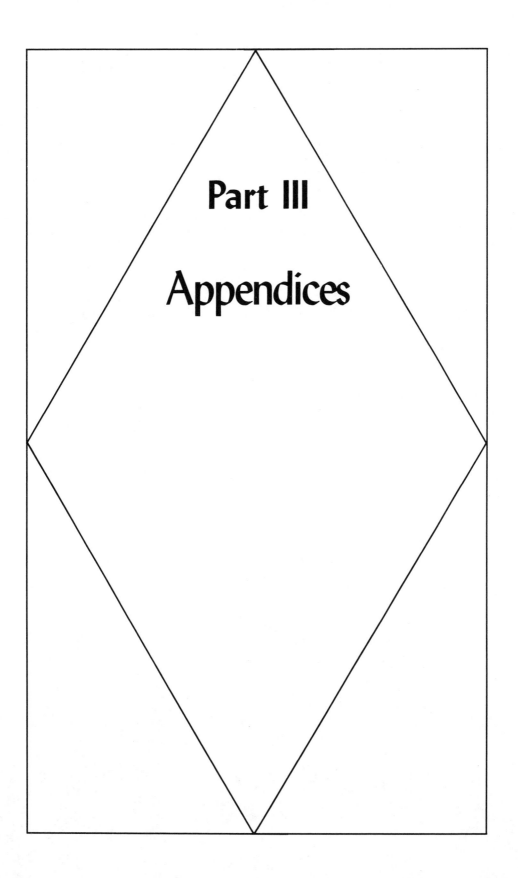

Part III

Appendices

Appendix A

Sample Scientific Subject Areas

The following is a listing of sample science project areas from various scientific fields that can be used to focus on possible project topics.

A

Acid/Environmental Studies

neutralization of
effects on wildlife
handling and transportation of
wood-pulp waste disposal
acid precipitation
acid soils

Acoustics

acoustic models
anechoic chambers
acoustics of music
noise control
sound holography
sound waves

Aerodynamics

wind tunnels
turbulence
drag study
hinge movements
in automobiles

Agriculture

feeds analysis
chemicals used in
effects of fertilizers
soil chemistry
pesticides used in farming

Air

effects of smog
effects of aerosols
airborne infections

Alcohol

alcoholism
as a fuel

Alloys

uses of: heat resistant and
electric/magnetic alloys

177

Amino Acids

function in man and animal
   metabolism of

Anesthesia

side effects of
comparative effects
between age groups

Animals

communication in
learning in/training of
effects on their migration
effects on their behavior

Antibiotics

analysis of
sources of
allergies to

Aquaculture

algae cultures
effects on fish hatcheries

Arteries

calcification of
prevention of disease in

Astronomy

satellite design
the moon's effects
effects of sunspots

Automobiles

modifications in
safety devices for

B

Bacteria

interaction in the body
as a toxin
needs for

Blood

clotting time of
diseases of
pigments in

Bones

composition of
abnormalities in
fractures in
diseases of

Botany

plant breeding
plant cloning
medicinal uses of

The Brain

abnormalities in
effects of injury on
diseases of

C

Cells

effects on cell division
effects on cell function

Chemicals

chemical bonds
chemical reactions
effects of toxic chemicals

Children

child development
child psychology
childhood disorders
learning disabilities in
sleeping needs of

Color

color perception
color variation
physiological effects of
psychological effects of
use in photography

H

Hair

effects of hair dyes/chemicals
transplantation of
effects of disease on

Health

effects of diet on
climatic effects on
medicinal effects on
analysis of exercises

Heart

effects of aging on
diseases of
effects of diet on
abnormalities in

Heat

insulation for
storage devices for
therapeutic uses of
as a disinfectant

Hydraulics

pumping modifications
turbine analyses
irrigation improvement
designs for

I

Ice

analysis of ice melters
effects on bacteria
effects on bodily tissues

Immune System

disorders of
effects of vaccinations on
diseases affecting

Infants

baby food/formula contents
behavior in
psychology of

Infrared Rays

image converters
industrial applications of
therapeutic uses of
effects of heating
effects on environment

Insects

communication between
foods of
as disease carriers
sterilization of
extermination of
uses of

Internal Combustion Engine

fuel consumption rates of
climatic effects on

Intestines

effects of bacteria in
effects of digestive aids in
diseases of
effects of diet on

L

Lasers

use in communications
use in surgery
use in photography

Lead

found in food
effects of its ingestion

Learning

influence of gender on
age factors in
learning disabilities
influence of diet on

Light

chemical actions of
psychological effects of
application in photography
therapeutic uses of

Lipids

metabolism of in man and animal
amount of lipids needed in diet

Liquids

viscosity comparisons
acoustics in

Lungs

effects of environment on
diseases of
abnormalities in

M

Magnetics

uses in instruments
uses in recording sound

Marine Engineering

ship propulsion
sea pollution control

Mathematics

found in nature
in computer programs

Metals

oxidation rates of
refining processes
effects of acids on

Meteorology

forecasting methods
weather controlling

Minerals

content in water
content in soil
uses in pharmacology
needed in nutrition

O

Ocean

waves as an energy source
effects of pollution on

Oil

refining modifications
effects on the environment
as a pesticide

Orthopedics

prosthetic device design
artificial joints
therapy after surgery

Oxygen

therapeutic uses of
industrial applications of

P

Parasites

prevention of
parasitic diseases
agricultural pests

Perception

in children/adults
disorders in
learning through

Pesticides

effects on the environment
containers for
biodegradation of

Photography

lens modification
uses in medicine
effects of temperature on

Plastics

effects on environment
effects of radiation on
uses in reconstructive surgery

Pollution

air and soil content
control of
control equipment analysis:
    purification devices or
    sewage disposals

Appendix B

U.S. Scientific Supply Companies

The following is a listing of 40 scientific supply companies from whom laboratory materials and other scientific supplies and apparatuses can be obtained. The companies shown here were selected because they specialize in equipment geared to science fair projects or as carrying equipment that is normally used in a school laboratory.

Northeast

Anachemia Chemical Inc.
3 Lincoln Blvd.
Rouses Point, NY 12979
800 323-1414

Baylis-American Co., Inc.
365 Charles St.
Providence, RI 02940
401 421-0828

Bowman-Mell & Co., Inc.
1334 Howard St.
Harrisburg, PA 17105
717 238-5235

Burrell Corp.
2223 Fifth Ave.
Pittsburgh, PA 15219
412 471-2527

Connecticut Valley Biological
    Supply Co.
82 Valley Rd.
Southampton, MA 01703
413 527-4030

Edmund Scientific
101 E. Gloucester Pike
Barrington, NJ 08007
609 573-6240

Learning Things, Inc.
P.O. Box 436
Arlington, MA 02174
617 646-0093

Macalaster Bicknell of CT, Inc.
181 Henry St.
New Haven, CT 06518
203 624-4191

Science Fair by ISSC
170–172 E. Main St.
Newark, DE 19711
302 453-1817

Science Kit, Inc.
777 E. Park Dr.
Tonawanda, NY 14150
716 874-6020

Central

American Science Center
5430 W. Layton Ave.
Milwaukee, WI 53220
414 281–2322

BME Lab Store
2459 University Ave. W
St. Paul, MN 55114
612 646–5339

Central Scientific
11222 Melrose Ave.
Franklin Park, IL 60131
708 451–0150

COE-PALM Biological Supply House
1130 N. Milwaukee Ave.
Chicago, IL 60606
312 486–2117

Fisher Scientific Co.
4901 W. LeMoyne St.
Chicago, IL 60651
800 642–1947

Frey Scientific Co.
905 Hickory Lane
Mansfield, OH 44905
419 589–9905

Harold J. Kloeppel & Associates
6100 N. Keystone Ave., Suite 403
Indianapolis, IN 46220
317 257–6955

Midland Scientific, Inc.
1202 S. 11th St.
Omaha, NE 68108
402 346–8352

Nasco
901 Jonesville Ave.
Fort Atkinson, WI 53538
414 563–2446

Science Explore Store
Science Museum of Minnesota
10th and Wabasha
St. Paul, MN 55101
612 221–4705

The Science Man Co.
4738 N. Harlem Ave.
Harwood Heights, IL 60656
708 867–4441

Science and Things
34781 Grand River
Farmington, MI 48024
313 478–8389

Southeast

Bartlett Chemicals, Inc.
4955 River Rd.
New Orleans, LA 70181
504 734–1971

Capitol Scientific, Inc.
2500 Rutland St.
Austin, TX 78766
512 836–1167

Carolina Biological Supply Co.
2700 York Rd.
Burlington, NC 27215
919 584–0381

M & M's Hobby, Art & Craft
1107 Veterans Memorial Blvd.
Metairie, LA 70005
504 833–3346

Rowlab Scientific
1650 Art Museum Dr.
Jacksonville, FL 32207
904 399–8036

Science Hobbies, Inc.
2615 Central Ave.
Charlotte, NC 28205
704 375–7684

Sun Scientific
175 SW 20th Way Dania
Tallahassee, FL 33004
800 330–1122

Universe of Science
2979 Emerald St.
Memphis, TN 38115
901 795–0882

Southwest

Chem Lab Supply
3221 E. Thomas Rd.
Tempe, AZ 85108
602 956–9550

Chem-Lab Supplies
1060-C Ortega Way
Placentia, CA 92670
714 630–7902

The Chem Shop
1151 S. Redwood Rd.
Salt Lake City, UT 84104
801 973–7966

Ed Tec Instruments
1859 W. 13070 S.
Riverton, UT 84065
801 254–2940

Lab Technologies
2227 S. 48th St., Suite F
Tempe, AZ 85202
602 431–1610

Martin's Star Tracker
633 S. Broadway
Boulder, CO 80303
303 499–0805

Tri-Ess Sciences
1020 Chestnut St.
Burbank, CA 91506
818 247–6910

Northwest

Carolina Biological Supply Co.
19375 McLouglin Blvd.
Gladstone, OR 97027
503 656–1641

Northwest Scientific, Inc.
15 N. 22nd
Billings, MT 59103
406 252–3269

Scientific Supply & Equipment
926 Poplar Place South
Seattle, WA 98144
206 324–8550

Appendix C_____

International Science and Engineering Fair Affiliates

There are currently over 350 affiliates of the International Science and Engineering Fair. Student finalists in grades 9 through 12 from these fairs are eligible to participate in this annual event administered by Science Service.

Below is a complete listing of all affiliated fairs and their hosting cities. Names, addresses, and telephone numbers of the fair directors and fair dates are not given because most change on a yearly basis. However, if you would like to have specific information about any of the listed fairs or one that is in your area, contact: Science Service, 1719 N Street, N.W., Washington, D.C. 20036; 203 785-2255.

UNITED STATES

Alabama

Alabama State Science and
   Engineering Fair, Decatur

Central Alabama Regional Science
   and Engineering Fair,
   Birmingham

East Alabama Regional Science Fair,
   Auburn

Mobile Regional Science Fair, Mobile

North Alabama Regional Science and
   Engineering Fair, Decatur

Northeast Alabama Regional Junior
   Science Fair, Talladega

West Alabama Regional Science Fair,
   Tuscaloosa

Alaska

Alaska Science and Engineering Fair,
   Anchorage

Arizona

Central Arizona Regional Science
   and Engineering Fair, Tempe

Northern Arizona Regional Science
   and Engineering Fair, Prescott

Southern Arizona Regional Science
   and Engineering Fair, Tucson

SSVEC's Youth Energy-Science Fair,
   Sierra Vista

Arkansas

Arkansas State Science Fair, Conway

Central Arkansas Regional Science Fair, Little Rock

North Central Arkansas Regional Science Fair, Batesville

Northeast Arkansas Regional Science Fair, Jonesboro

Northwest Arkansas Regional Science and Engineering Fair, Fayetteville

South Central Arkansas Regional Science Fair, Arkadelphia

Southeast Arkansas Regional Science Fair, Monticello

Southwest Arkansas Regional Science Fair, Camden

California

Alhambra Science and Engineering Expo, Alhambra

California Central Valleys Science and Engineering Fair, Fresno

California Central Valleys Science and Engineering Fair, Modesto

California Central Valleys Science and Engineering Fair, Sacramento

Greater San Diego Science and Engineering Fair, San Diego

Monterey County Science and Engineering Fair, Monterey

Robert A. Millikan Science and Engineering Fair, San Gabriel

San Francisco Bay Area Science Fair, San Francisco

Santa Clara Valley Science and Engineering Fair, San Jose

Colorado

Arkansas Valley Regional Science Fair, Rocky Ford

Colorado State Science Fair, Fort Collins

Denver Metropolitan Science Fair, Golden

Longs Peak Science and Engineering Fair, Greeley

Morgan-Washington Bi-County Science Fair, Brush

National American Indian Science Fair, Boulder

Pikes Peak Regional Science Fair, Colorado Springs

San Luis Valley Regional Science Fair, Alamosa

Western Colorado Science Fair, Grand Junction

Connecticut

Connecticut State Science Fair, Hartford

District of Columbia

District of Columbia Citywide Science Fair, Washington, D.C.

Florida

Alachua Region Science and Engineering Fair, Gainesville

Big Springs Regional Science Fair, Ocala

Brevard Islands Science and Engineering Fair, Merritt Island

Brevard Mainland Science and Engineering Fair, Titusville

Brevard South-Indian River Science and Engineering Fair, Melbourne

Capital Regional Science and Engineering Fair, Tallahassee

Chipola Regional Science and Engineering Fair, Marianna

Citrus Regional Science and Engineering Fair, Crystal River

East Broward County Science Fair, Hollywood

Florida State Science and
Engineering Fair, St.
Petersburg

Florida Three Rivers Science and
Engineering Fair, Panama City

Hernando County Regional Science
and Engineering Fair–East,
Brooksville

Hernando County Regional Science
and Engineering Fair–West,
Brooksville

Hillsborough Regional Science Fair,
Tampa

Lake County School's Curriculum
Fair, Leesburg

Lakeland Regional Science and
Engineering Fair, Lakeland

Manatee Regional Science and
Engineering Fair, Bradenton

Martin County Regional Science and
Engineering Fair, Stuart

Northeast Florida Kiwanis Regional
Science and Engineering Fair,
Jacksonville

Northeast Panhandle Regional
Science and Engineering Fair,
Fort Walton Beach

Orange County Regional Science and
Engineering Fair, Orlando

Palm Beach County Science and
Engineering Fair, West Palm
Beach

Pasco Regional Science and
Engineering Fair, Hudson

Pinellas Regional Science and
Engineering Fair, St.
Petersburg

Polk County Regional Science and
Engineering Fair, Lakeland

Putnam Regional Science and
Engineering Fair, Palatka

River Region East Science Fair, St.
Augustine

Seminole County Regional Science
Fair, Sanford

Southeast Panhandle Regional
Science and Engineering Fair,
Fort Walton Beach

South Florida Science and
Engineering Fair, Miami

Space Coast Science and Engineering
Fair, Cocoa Beach

Space Congress Youth Science and
Engineering Fair, Cocoa Beach

Sumter County Regional Science
Fair, Ocala

Suwanee Valley Regional Science
and Engineering Fair, Lake
City

Thomas Alva Edison East Regional
Science Fair, Fort Myers

Thomas Alva Edison Regional
Science Fair, Fort Myers

Tomoka Region Science and
Engineering Fair, Daytona
Beach

Treasure Coast Regional Science and
Engineering Fair, Fort Pierce

West Broward County Science Fair,
Hollywood

West Panhandle Regional Science
and Engineering Fair,
Pensacola

Georgia

Atlanta Science and Mathematics
Congress, Atlanta

Calhoun Area Regional Science and
Engineering Fair, Calhoun

Coastal Georgia Regional Science
and Engineering Fair,
Brunswick

Darton College Regional Science
Fair, Albany

First Congressional District Science
and Engineering Fair,
Savannah

Georgia State Science and
Engineering Fair, Athens

Oconee RESA/Georgia College
Regional Science and
Engineering Fair, Milledgeville

Hawaii

Hawaii Association of Independent
Schools Science and
Engineering Fair, Honolulu

Hawaii District Science and
Engineering Fair, Honolulu

Hawaii State Science and
Engineering Fair, Honolulu

Idaho

Lewis-Clark Regional Science and
Engineering Fair, Lewiston

Illinois

Chicago Public Schools Student
Science Fair–Region I,
Chicago

Chicago Public Schools Student
Science Fair–Region II,
Chicago

Heart of Illinois Science and
Engineering Fair, Peoria

Illinois Junior Academy of Science
Region X Science Fair,
Springfield

Illinois Junior Academy of Science
Region XII Science Fair,
Edwardsville

Indiana

Calumet Regional Science Fair,
Hammond

Central Indiana Regional Science
and Engineering Fair,
Indianapolis

East Central Indiana Regional
Science Fair, Muncie

Lafayette Regional Science and
Engineering Fair, West
Lafayette

Northeastern Indiana Regional
Science and Engineering Fair,
Fort Wayne

Northeastern Indiana Tri-State
Regional Science Fair, Angola

Northern Indiana Regional Science
Fair, South Bend

Northwestern Indiana Science and
Engineering Fair, Westville

South Central Indiana Regional
Science and Engineering Fair,
Bloomington

Southeastern Indiana Regional
Science Fair, New Albany

Tri-State Regional Science and
Engineering Fair, Evansville

West Central Indiana Regional
Science and Engineering Fair,
Terre Haute

Iowa

Eastern Iowa Science and
Engineering Fair, Cedar Rapids

Greater Quad City Area Science and
Engineering Fair–Illinois
Section, Davenport

Greater Quad City Area Science and
Engineering Fair–Iowa
Section, Davenport

Iowa Hawkeye Science Fair, West
Des Moines

Northeast Iowa Science and
Engineering Fair, Fayette

South Central Iowa Science and
Engineering Fair, Indianola

Kansas

Wamego Regional Science Fair,
Wamego

Kentucky

Cumberland College Regional
Science Fair, Williamsburg

Louisville Regional Science Fair,
Louisville

Murray State University Regional
Science Fair, Murray

Northeast Kentucky Regional
Science Fair, Morehead

Southern Kentucky Regional Science
Fair, Bowling Green

Louisiana

Capitol District Region VII Science
and Engineering Fair, Baton
Rouge

Greater New Orleans Science and
Engineering Fair, New Orleans

Louisiana Region I Science and
Engineering Fair, Bossier City

Louisiana Region II Science and
Engineering Fair, Ruston

Louisiana Region III Science and
Engineering Fair, Monroe

Louisiana Region V Science and
Engineering Fair, Lake Charles

Louisiana Region VIII Science and
Engineering Fair, Hammond

Louisiana Region X Science and
Engineering Fair, Thibodaux,
Louisiana

Louisiana State Science and
Engineering Fair, Baton Rouge,
Louisiana

St. James Parish Science Fair,
Lutcher, Louisiana

Terrebonne Parish Science Fair,
Houma, Louisiana

University of Southwestern
Louisiana Region VI Science
Fair, Lafayette, Louisiana

Maryland

Anne Arundel County Science and
Engineering Fair, Arnold

Baltimore Science Fair, Towson

Frederick County Science and
Engineering Fair, Frederick

Montgomery Area Science Fair,
Gaithersburg

Prince George's Area Science Fair,
Largo

Washington County Science and
Engineering Fair, Hagerstown

Western Maryland Regional Science
Expo, McHenry

Massachusetts

Massachusetts Region IV Science
Fair, Somerville

Massachusetts Region V Science Fair,
Bridgewater

Massachusetts State Science Fair,
Cambridge

Michigan

Flint Area Science Fair, Flint

Saginaw County Science and
Engineering Fair, Saginaw

Science and Engineering Fair of
Metropolitan Detroit, Inc.–#1,
Detroit

Science and Engineering Fair of
Metropolitan Detroit, Inc.–#2,
Detroit

Science and Engineering Fair of
Metropolitan Detroit, Inc.–#3,
Detroit

Science and Engineering Fair of
Metropolitan Detroit, Inc.–#4,
Detroit

Southeastern Michigan Science Fair,
Ann Arbor

Minnesota

Central Minnesota Regional Science
Fair and Research Paper
Program, St. Cloud

Minnesota State Science Fair and
Research Paper Program,
Moorhead

Northeast Minnesota Regional
Science Fair, Duluth

Northern Minnesota Regional
Science Fair, Bemidji

Rochester Public Schools Science
Fair, Rochester

South Central/North Minnesota
Regional Science and
Engineering Fair, Mankato

South Central/South Minnesota
Regional Science and
Engineering Fair, Mankato

Southeast Minnesota Regional
Science Fair, Rochester

Southwest/North Minnesota
Regional Science and
Engineering Fair, Mankato

Southwest/South Minnesota
Regional Science and
Engineering Fair, Mankato

Twin Cities Regional Science Fair,
Minneapolis

Western Minnesota Regional Science
Fair, Moorhead

Mississippi

Mississippi Region I Science and
Engineering Fair, Hattiesburg

Mississippi Region II Science and
Engineering Fair, Jackson

Mississippi Region III Science and
Engineering Fair, Cleveland

Mississippi Region IV Science Fair,
Booneville

Mississippi Region V–North Science
and Engineering Fair,
Mississippi State

Mississippi Region V–South Science
and Engineering Fair,
Mississippi State

Mississippi Region VI Science and
Engineering Fair, Biloxi

Mississippi Region VII Science and
Engineering Fair, University of
Mississippi

Mississippi State Science and
Engineering Fair, Jackson

Missouri

Greater Kansas City Science and
Engineering Fair, Kansas City

Greater Springfield Area Science
Fair, Springfield

Greater St. Louis Science Fair,
Manchester

Lincoln University Regional Science
Fair, Jefferson City

Mid-America Regional Science and
Engineering Fair, St. Joseph

Missouri Southern Regional Science
Fair, Joplin

Northeast Missouri Regional Science
and Engineering Fair,
Kirksville

South Central Missouri Regional
Science and Engineering Fair,
Rolla

Southeast Missouri Regional Science
Fair, Cape Girardeau

St. Charles-Lincoln Science Fair,
O'Fallon

Montana

Montana Region II Science and
Engineering Fair, Great Falls

Montana Science Fair, Missoula

Southwestern Montana Regional
Science and Engineering Fair,
Butte

Nebraska

Central Nebraska Science and
Engineering Fair, Franklin

Greater Nebraska Science and
Engineering Fair, Nebraska
City

Nevada

Elko County Science Fair, Elko

Southern Nevada Science Fair, Las
Vegas

Western Nevada Regional Science
Fair, Reno

New Jersey

Greater Trenton Science and
Engineering Fair, Trenton

Hudson County Science Fair,
Hoboken

North Jersey Regional Science Fair,
Morristown

New Mexico

Four Corners New Mexico Regional
Science and Engineering Fair,
Grants

New Mexico Science and
Engineering Fair, Socorro

Northeastern New Mexico Regional
Science and Engineering Fair,
Las Vegas

Northwestern New Mexico Regional
Science and Engineering Fair,
Albuquerque

San Juan New Mexico Regional
Science and Engineering Fair,
Farmington

Southeastern New Mexico Regional
Science and Engineering Fair,
Portales

Southwestern New Mexico Regional
Science and Engineering Fair,
Las Cruces

New York

Allegheny Mountain Science Fair,
Olean

Dutchess County Regional Science
Fair, Poughkeepsie

Greater Syracuse Scholastic Science
Fair, Syracuse

Long Island Science and Engineering
Fair, Stony Brook

New York Academy of Sciences/
American Institute School
Science Fair, Bronx, New York

New York Academy of Sciences/
American Institute School
Science Fair, Brooklyn, New
York

New York Academy of Sciences/
American Institute School
Science Fair, Manhattan, New
York

New York Academy of Sciences/
American Institute School
Science Fair, Queens, New
York

New York Academy of Sciences/
American Institute School
Science Fair, Staten Island,
New York

Tarrytown Regional Science and
Engineering Fair, North
Tarrytown

Utica College Regional Science Fair,
Utica

North Carolina

Mecklenburg County Science,
Mathematics and Engineering
Fair, Charlotte

Southwest North Carolina Regional
Science, Mathematics and
Engineering Fair, Charlotte

North Dakota

North Central North Dakota
Regional Science and
Engineering Fair, Devils Lake

North Dakota State Science and
Engineering Fair, Fargo

Northeast North Dakota Regional
Science and Engineering Fair,
Hillsboro

Northwest Central North Dakota
Regional Science Fair, Minot

Northwest North Dakota Regional
Science Fair, Williston

Southeast Central North Dakota Regional Science and Engineering Fair, Jamestown

Southeast North Dakota Regional Science and Engineering Fair, Mayville

Southwest Central North Dakota Regional Science and Engineering Fair, Bismark

Southwest North Dakota Regional Science and Engineering Fair, Hettinger

Ohio

Ada Regional Science and Engineering Fair, Ada

Buckeye Science and Engineering Fair, Delaware

Dayton Science and Engineering Fair, Dayton

Hugo H. and Mabel B. Young Science and Engineering Fair, Millersburg

Lake-to-River Science and Engineering Fair, Youngstown

Marietta Regional Science and Engineering Fair, Marietta

Marion Science and Engineering Fair, Marion

Montgomery County Science and Engineering Fair, Dayton

Northeastern Ohio Science and Engineering Fair, Cleveland

Northwest Ohio Science and Engineering Fair, Hamler

Ohio Academy of Sciences District XIII Science Day, North Canton

Otterbein-Battelle Regional Science Fair, Westerville

Southeastern Ohio Regional Science and Engineering Fair, Athens

Southwestern Ohio Science and Engineering Fair, Oxford

Western Reserve Science Day, Akron

Oklahoma

Bartlesville District Science Fair, Bartlesville

Cameron University Regional Science Fair, Lawton

Central Oklahoma Regional Science Fair, Edmond

East Central Oklahoma Regional Science and Engineering Fair, Seminole

Eastern Oklahoma Regional Science and Engineering Fair, Wilburton

Muskogee Regional Science and Engineering Fair, Muskogee

Northeastern Oklahoma A&M Science and Engineering Fair, Miami

Northwestern Oklahoma State University Regional Science Fair, Alva

Oklahoma City Regional Science and Engineering Fair, Oklahoma City

Oklahoma State Science and Engineering Fair, Ada

Southeastern Oklahoma District Science and Engineering Fair, Ardmore

Tulsa Regional Science and Engineering Fair, Tulsa

Oregon

Northwest Science Exposition, Portland

Southwestern Oregon Regional Science Exposition, Gold Beach

Pennsylvania

Ben Franklin Science Fair, Philadelphia

Benjamin Banneker Science Fair, Philadelphia

Capital Area Science and
Engineering Fair, Carlisle

Delaware Valley Science Fair,
Philadelphia

Lancaster Science and Engineering
Fair, Lancaster

Marie Curie Science Fair,
Philadelphia

Pittsburgh Regional Science and
Engineering Fair, Pittsburgh

Reading and Berks Science and
Engineering Fair, Reading

York County Science and
Engineering Fair, York

Rhode Island

Rhode Island State Science Fair,
Warwick

South Carolina

Central Savannah River Area Science
and Engineering Fair, Aiken

Low County Science Fair, Charleston

Piedmont South Carolina Region III
Science Fair, Spartanburg

Sand Hills Region IV Science Fair,
Florence

Sea Island Regional Science Fair,
Beaufort

South Carolina Region II Science
Fair, Columbia

Western South Carolina Region I
Science Fair, Greenville

South Dakota

Eastern South Dakota Science and
Engineering Fair, Brookings

High Plains Regional Science and
Engineering Fair, Rapid City

Northern South Dakota Science and
Math Fair, Aberdeen

Northwest Area Schools Regional
Science and Engineering Fair,
Timber Lake

Tennessee

Chattanooga Regional Science and
Engineering Fair, Chattanooga

Cumberland Plateau Science and
Engineering Fair, Cookeville

Memphis-Shelby County Science and
Engineering Fair–East Region,
Memphis

Memphis-Shelby County Science and
Engineering Fair–North
Region, Memphis

Memphis-Shelby County Science and
Engineering Fair–South
Region, Memphis

Middle Tennessee Science and
Engineering Fair, Nashville

Southern Appalachian Science and
Engineering Fair, Knoxville

West Tennessee Regional Science
Fair, Jackson

Texas

Alamo Regional Science and
Engineering Fair–I, San
Antonio

Alamo Regional Science and
Engineering Fair–II, San
Antonio

Austin Area Science and Engineering
Fair, Austin

Brazos Valley Regional Science and
Engineering Fair, College
Station

Central Texas Regional Science Fair,
Waco

Coastal Bend Science and
Engineering Competition,
Corpus Christi

Dallas Morning News Regional
Science and Engineering Fair,
Dallas

District XI Texas Science Fair, San
Angelo

East Texas Regional Science Fair,
Kilgore

Fort Worth Regional Science Fair,
Fort Worth

High Plains Regional Science Fair,
Amarillo

Laredo Independent School District
Science Fair, Laredo

Midwestern State University
Regional Science and
Engineering Fair, Wichita Falls

Permian Basin Regional Science Fair,
Odessa

Rio Grande Valley Regional Science
Fair, Harlingen

Science Engineering Fair of Houston,
Houston

South Plains Regional Science and
Engineering Fair, Lubbock

Spring Science Competition, Abilene

Sun Country Science Fair, El Paso

Texas Mid-Coast Regional Science
and Engineering Fair, Victoria

Texas State Science and Engineering
Fair, Austin

United Independent School District
Regional Science Fair, Laredo

Utah

Box Elder Science and Engineering
Fair, Brigham City

Central Utah Science and
Engineering Fair, Provo

Color Country Utah Science and
Engineering Fair, Cedar City

North Davis Area Science Fair,
Bountiful

North Weber Area Science and
Engineering Fair, Pleasant
View

Ogden Area I Science and
Engineering Fair, Ogden

Roy Area Science and Engineering
Fair, Roy

Salt Lake Metropolitan Science Fair,
Salt Lake City

South Central Utah Regional Science
and Engineering Fair, Cedar
City

South Davis Area Science and
Engineering Fair, Bountiful

Southeastern Utah Regional Science
and Engineering Fair, Blanding

Southern Utah Science and
Engineering Fair, Cedar City

South Weber Regional Science and
Engineering Fair, Ogden

Southwest Utah Science and
Engineering Fair, Cedar City

State Science and Engineering Fair of
Utah, Ogden

Virginia

Central Virginia Regional Science
Fair, Lynchburg

Fairfax County Area I Regional
Science and Engineering Fair,
Fairfax

Fairfax County Area II Regional
Science and Engineering Fair,
Fairfax

Fairfax County Area III Regional
Science and Engineering Fair,
Fairfax

Fairfax County Area IV Regional
Science and Engineering Fair,
Fairfax

Fairfax County Regional Science and
Engineering Fair–Thomas
Jefferson High School for
Science and Technology,
Fairfax

James River Regional Science Fair,
Hopewell

Loudoun County Regional Science
Fair, Ashburn

Northern Virginia Science and
Engineering Fair, Arlington

Piedmont Regional Science Fair,
Charlottesville

Prince William-Manassas Regional
Science Fair, Nokesville

Shenandoah Valley Regional Science
Fair, Harrisonburg

Southside Virginia Regional Science
Fair, Farmville

Southwestern Virginia Regional
Science Fair, Wise

Tidewater Science Fair, Tabb

Virginia State Science and
Engineering Fair, Sterling

Western Virginia Regional Science
Fair, Roanoke

Washington

Mid-Columbia Regional Science and
Engineering Fair, Kennewick

Washington State Science and
Engineering Fair, Bremerton

West Virginia

Central West Virginia Regional
Science and Engineering Fair,
Montgomery

Mercer County Science and
Engineering Fair, Athens

West Liberty State College Regional
Science and Engineering Fair,
West Liberty

West Virginia Eastern Regional
Science Fair, Keyser

West Virginia State Science and
Engineering Fair, Glenville

WVU-P Western Regional Science
and Engineering Fair,
Parkersburg

Wisconsin

Southeastern Wisconsin Science and
Engineering Fair, Milwaukee

Wyoming

Southeast Wyoming Regional
Science Fair, Cheyenne

Wyoming State Science Fair,
Sheridan

FAIRS HELD OUTSIDE THE U.S.

American Samoa

American Samoa Science Fair, Utulci

Canada (Ontario)

Hamilton District Science and
Engineering Fair, Hamilton

Niagara Regional Science and
Engineering Fair, St.
Catherines

Guam

Guam Island-Wide Science Fair,
Mangilao

Ireland

Aer Lingus Young Scientists
Exhibition, Dublin

Japan

Japan Students Science Awards,
Tokyo

Puerto Rico

Arecibo Regional Science Fair,
Arecibo

Bayamon Regional Science Fair,
Bayamon

Caguas Educational Region Science
Fair I, Arroyo

Caguas Educational Region Science
Fair II, Arroyo

Caguas Educational Region Science
Fair III, Arroyo

Caguas Educational Region Science
Fair IV, Arroyo

Eastern Regional Mathematics Fair,
San Juan

Humacao Regional Science Fair I,
Ceiba

Humacao Regional Science Fair II,
Ceiba

Mayaguez Educational Region
Science Fair I, San German

Mayaguez Educational Region
Science Fair II, San German

Mayaguez Educational Region
Science Fair III, San German

Mayaguez Educational Region
Science Fair IV, San German

Mayaguez Educational Region
Science Fair V, San German

Mayaguez Educational Region
Science Fair VI, San German

Mayaguez Educational Region
Science Fair VII, San German

Mayaguez Educational Region
Science Fair VIII, San German

Mayaguez Educational Region
Science Fair IX, San German

Ponce Regional Science Fair I, Ponce

Ponce Regional Science Fair II,
Ponce

Ponce Regional Science Fair III,
Ponce

Ponce Regional Science Fair IV,
Ponce

Private School Consortium Science
and Engineering Fair, Cayey

Puerto Rico State Science Fair I, San
German

Puerto Rico State Science Fair II, San
German

San Juan Archdiocesan Region I
Science Fair, Rio Piedras

San Juan Archdiocesan Region II
Science Fair, Rio Piedras

San Juan Archdiocesan Region III
Science Fair, Rio Piedras

San Juan Educational Region Science
Fair I, San Juan

San Juan Educational Region Science
Fair II, San Juan

San Juan Educational Region Science
Fair III, San Juan

San Juan Educational Region Science
Fair IV, San Juan

Western Bayamon Regional Science
Fair, Bayamon

Western Regional Mathematics Fair,
Aquadilla

Republic of China

Middle Taiwan Regional Science
Fair, Taichung

Republic of China (Taiwan) National
Science and Engineering Fair,
Taipei

South Taiwan Regional Science Fair,
Tainan

Sweden

Utställningen Unga Forskare,
Stockholm

United Kingdom

British Association Science and
Technology Fair, London

198

Glossary

abstract A brief summary of the science project (approx. 250 words) that explains the project's objective and procedure and provides generalized data and a workable solution to the problem addressed by the project.

backboard A self-supporting bulletin board with a summary outline of a science project. The backboard contains the project title and topic progression, together with flow charts, photographs, and other significant project descriptions. The backboard is usually organized according to the scientific method.

biological category A basic category encompassing several life sciences, including behavioral and social sciences, biochemistry, botany, ecology, genetics, medicine and health, microbiology, zoology, animal species studies, disease, etc.

clarity A judging criterion that checks to see if a science project is presented in a concise fashion.

conclusion The solution to a proposed issue and confirmation or rejection of a hypothesis.

control A part of an experiment that provides a guideline for comparing an experimental group.

creative ability A criteria used in judging that grades ingenuity and originality in an approach to a topic.

data Recorded information that is organized for final analysis and observation.

dependent variable The variable that is being measured.

display The complete set-up of a science project. The display includes a backboard, a representation of the subject matter or experimental results, and a research report.

dramatic value A criterion used in judging that determines whether the project is presented in a way that attracts attention through the use of graphics and layouts.

erroneous hypothesis An incorrect or vague hypothesis that does not support the experimental results.

experiment   The part of the project where the scientist tests to verify a law, explain a cause-and-effect relationship, measure efficiency, or observe an unexplained process.

experimental angle   The narrowed experimental option best suited to bringing about a desired or fitting solution to the issue.

frequency distribution   A mathematical summary of a set of data that shows the numerical frequency of each class of items.

frequency polygon   A graph that represents a frequency distribution. Item class midpoints are found and plotted at a point in correspondence to their accompanying frequency.

histogram   A graph that represents a frequency distribution. The item classes are placed along the horizontal axis and the frequencies along the vertical axis. Rectangles are drawn with the item class as the base and frequency as the side.

hypothesis   The assumed or tentative guess as to the possible solution to a problem.

independent variable   The variable that is controlled or manipulated by the experimenter.

journal   A logbook used to record everything that the student has learned and completed with his or her project. Items to note include articles read, places visited, data results, etc.

line graph   A graph used to summarize information from a table. It has an x (horizontal) axis and a y (vertical) axis, where points are plotted at corresponding regions.

mean   The measurement of the central location of a group of data through the use of a mathematical average. The mean is denoted by the symbol $(\overline{x})$.

percentile   The position of one value from a set of data that expresses the percentage of the other data that lie below this value. The value of a particular percentile can be calculated by dividing the desired percentile by 100 and multiplying by the number of items in the ascending data set.

physical category   A basic category including chemistry, math, earth and space science, engineering, physics, toxic waste, electronics, etc.

pie chart   A graph represented by a circle that is divided into segments. The circle represents the whole amount (100%), and each section represents a percentage of the whole.

primary sources   Those sources of information that consist of surveys, observations, and experiments done directly by the science student.

procedural plan   A uniform and systematic way of testing the subject matter. Procedural planning begins with correlating to determine variables and a uniform control group.

project limitation guidelines   Guidelines established by the ISEF that explain how far a student may go in his or her research and experimentation.

project display   The item(s) from the science project that can fully represent, exemplify or explain research, experimentation, and conclusions.

purpose/objective   The goal of a project, the theme that requires greater development or understanding.

research   The process by which information about the issue at hand is collected to search for possible clues in the development of the purpose or objective.

200

research report An in-depth discussion of an entire science project from start to finish, including a subject history, research experience, method applied, experimental angle used, data, conclusive remarks, glossary, photos, diagrams, etc.

science fair An exhibition of selectively chosen science projects grouped into corresponding categories and marked for their quality. Science fairs occur on local, state, regional, and international levels. (The fairs discussed in this book refer to those affiliated with the International Science and Engineering Fair.)

science project A project of scientific nature that is done by a grade student for a local, state, regional, or international science exhibition. The project employs a systematic approach in order to formulate a conclusion to a proposed scientific question. The science project is modeled after the scientific method.

scientific abstracts Bound volumes of thousands of brief scientific discussions. Scientific abstracts are grouped into two classes: research and experimental. The abstracts discuss experimental reports and review scientific literature.

scientific method An organized process used for developing a solution to answer a specific question.

scientific thought A criterion used in judging that is based on how a science project shows evidence of an applied scientific or engineering development through cause-and-effect, verification of laws, applied techniques for efficiency, or presentation of a new concept.

secondary sources Sources of information written by outsiders and obtained through libraries, media, government agencies, or corporations.

skill A criteria used in judging that grades a science project on how much scientific and engineering practice was employed. The level of experimentation, preparation, and treatment of the subject matter play an important role.

statistical method A method used to further describe and summarize data results through the use of specialized numbers, graphs, and charts.

table An orderly display of data, usually arranged in rows and columns.

tests and surveys The techniques that try to determine the relationship, if any, that exists between variables and measures the closeness of this relationship.

thoroughness A criteria used in judging that checks the variety and depth of the literature used, experimental investigation, and all the aspects of the project.

variable Some characteristic of an object, environment, plant, animal, performance, or behavior that can take on two or more values.

Index

Hard water respiration
  see Mealworms
Hypothesis, 10, 19, 20, 28
  see also Scientific method

I

Ice melters, 60–61
Independent variable, 20–21
Insulation materials, 78–79
International Science and Engineering Fair
  awards, 39
  display restrictions, 33
  guidelines for experimentation, 15
  judging, 39
  Science Service, 40
ISEF
  see International Science and Engineering Fair

J

Journal, 14, 21, 32
Judges, 9, 36, 37, 38
Judging, 36–39

K

Kitchen cleaning materials
  see Bacteria analyses

L

Letter writing, 16
Limestone
  see Acid rain
Lobster shell chitin
  see Metals

M

Mass, calculation of, 69
Mealworms
  effects of caffeine on, 113–115

Mealworms (*Contd.*)
  hard and soft water respiration in, 163–164
  locomotion on different surfaces, 165–166
Mean
  see Statistics
Metals
  corrosion of, 62–63
  metallic absorption by lobster shell chitin, 64–66

O

Ocean waves, use of in generating electricity, 76–77
Oil spills, effect of on plants, 91–92
Origami and golden mean/ratio, 116–119

P

Paper bags, biodegradability of, 97–98
Paper chromatography with dyes, 73–75
Pendulums, 145–147
Percentile
  see Statistics
Periodicals
  see Research
pH levels, 62–63, 99–101, 106–107
Pie chart
  see Graphs
Plants
  cancer in, 54–56
  cloning of, 52–53
  effect of acid rain on, 93–94
  oil spills and, 91–92
  transpiration in, 49–51
Plastic bags, biodegradability of, 97–98
Polariscope, 153–155
Presenting a project
  in an interview, 38–39
  see also Judging
Protista, 15
P-Trap
  see Bacteria analyses